Odoevsky's four pathways into modern fiction

Manchester University Press

Odoevsky's four pathways into modern fiction

A comparative study

NEIL CORNWELL

Manchester University Press
MANCHESTER AND NEW YORK

distributed in the United States exclusively by Palgrave Macmillan

Published by Manchester University Press
Oxford Road, Manchester M13 9NR, UK
and Room 400, 175 Fifth Avenue, New York, NY 10010, USA
www.manchesteruniversitypress.co.uk

Distributed in the United States exclusively by
Palgrave Macmillan, 175 Fifth Avenue, New York,
NY 10010, USA

Distributed in Canada exclusively by
UBC Press, University of British Columbia, 2029 West Mall,
Vancouver, BC, Canada V6T 1Z2

British Library Cataloguing-in-Publication Data
A catalogue record for this book is available from the British Library

Library of Congress Cataloging-in-Publication Data applied for

ISBN 978 0 7190 8209 2 hardback

First published 2010

The publisher has no responsibility for the persistence or accuracy of URLs
for any external or third-party internet websites referred to in this book, and
does not guarantee that any content on such websites is, or will remain,
accurate or appropriate.

Typeset
by Toppan Best-set Premedia Limited
Printed in Great Britain
by MPG Books Group, UK

Contents

Preface

You know, the more I think about it, the more I realize that literature only exists for one reason: it saves writers from being disgusted with life.

(J.-K. Huysmans, *The Damned [Là-Bas]*)

The present modest volume, entitled *Odoevsky's Four Pathways into Modern Fiction: A Comparative Study*, contains four chapters entitled 'Musicman', 'Starman', 'Seerman' and 'Monk'.

This might-have-been quartet of occupational categories (with apologies to John Le Carré, Ellery Queen and wherever the 'Rich man, poor man . . .' counting game originates) masks the more or less (as the case may be) obvious callings of musician, astronaut, psychic detective and, . . . well . . . , monk. What, if anything, might there be to link such a grouping?

As the title may go some way to suggest, the project treats in turn four stories by the Russian Romantic-Gothic writer Vladimir Odoevsky (1804–1869). The intention is to demonstrate the particular suitability of these four works as jumping-off points for four trends, or subgenres, in fiction, and then to make analytical use of these categories. These extend from the Romantic era (which means the 1830s and early 1840s, in Odoevsky's Russia) – taking appropriate note of relevant previous examples or traditions – into later Russian, and indeed overall largely comparative, fictional realms. Hence the notion of 'pathways' into fiction. Dosto-evsky can also be seen to play a key role, at least in two of these four cases. The categories featured are, in titular order: the artistic-musical story; the development of narratives of some form of purported interstellar travel, assisting in the rise of science fiction; the phenomenon of the psychic detective; and, finally, certain aspects (largely here to do with duels) connected with the confessional element within the novel, seen mainly through the disclosures of monastic inmates.

While the 'Musicman' and 'Starman' chapters here may represent relatively limited paradigms of their themes, in terms both of texts or authors examined and chronological span, both 'Seerman' and 'Monk' do, comparatively speaking, take wings. Although focusing their main analyses well within the nineteenth century, they also reach forward (without making any undue claims for comprehensiveness) to the fiction of the present day.

Acknowledgements

Thanks are due, for information or materials supplied, or suggestions made, to: Michael Basker, Leon Burnett, Carla De Petris, David Gillespie, Terry Hale, William Hughes, Ron Knowles, Aleksandr Koren'kov, Maggie Malone, Richard Peace, Ian Press, Robert Reid, Claire Whitehead.

Versions of the first two chapters have appeared (in 2008) as follows:

'The musical-artistic story: Hoffmann, Odoevsky and Pasternak', *Comparative Critical Studies*, 5, 1, 2008, pp. 35–55.

'The rise of the "cosmic traveller": Odoevsky, Dostoevsky, Hodgson, Stapledon', in *Russian Literature and the West: A Tribute for David M. Bethea*, Part I, ed. Alexander Dolinin, Lazar Fleishman and Leonid Livak, Stanford: Stanford Slavic Studies, 2008, pp. 252–66.

N.C.

Introduction

Life is not recountable, and it seems extraordinary that men have spent all the centuries we know anything about devoted to doing just that, determined to tell what cannot be told, be it in the form of myth, epic poem, chronicle, annals, minutes, legend or *chanson de geste*, ballad or folk-song, gospel, hagiography, history, biography, novel or funeral oration, film, confession, memoir, article, it makes no difference.

(Javier Marías, *Your Face Tomorrow.*
1: Fever and Spear [*Tu rostro mañana. 1: Fiebre y lanza*])

The present project, as may already be apparent from the Preface, grew, largely and eventually, from my preoccupation over a period of time with the fantastic in literature (first primarily Russian and then, increasingly, comparative), which in turn had stemmed from work on Vladimir Odoevsky. This work developed to involve biographical research, criticism and translation. My interest in this originated during my undergraduate years, and grew to a considerable extent from a fascination with the fiction (and the impact) of E.T.A. Hoffmann, and from the discovery (in the School of Slavonic and East European Studies Library) of a pioneering book called *The Russian Hoffmannists* – one which included a chapter on 'Prince Odoevskij, the Philosopher'.[1] Such tentative beginnings were, a little later, driven into some sort of initial focus by an entirely fortuitous invitation from a publisher to supply an introduction to a (western) reprint of a valuable and neglected edition of Odoevsky's 'Romantic Tales'.[2] This in turn led on to a translation of, and then an article featuring, Odoevsky's *The Live Corpse* (a story now appearing once again in the second chapter here). This sequence need be taken no further, at least for the present.

*   *   *   *   *

The first chapter of this study, 'Musicman: the musical-artistic story from Hoffmann and Odoevsky to Pasternak', investigates the musical story through Odoevsky's fictional 'biography' of Johann Sebastian Bach, and preceding works, particularly in the writings of E.T.A. Hoffmann. The purpose is then to examine an early prose work by Boris Pasternak, his *Suboctave Story* (written in 1916–17, but first published only in 1977). Pasternak's never quite completed novella, it is argued, may be dependent to a considerable extent on Odoevsky's depiction of the young Bach and his creation of musical atmosphere.

The second chapter is 'Starman: the rise of the "cosmic traveller"'. Here the motif of round-the-world flight, and the impact on surrounding society of the quirks of a single life, in Odoevsky's tale *The Live Corpse*, is seen to be developed into what purports to be interplanetary flight, and the rise and fall of a civilisation, in Dostoevsky's late story *The Dream of a Ridiculous Man* (followed by a Futurist poetic touch from Vladimir Maiakovsky). Particulars of such supposed cosmic (or astral) travel may have been, in part at least, 'borrowed' by his successors from Dostoevsky. However this may be, such things are seen to be taken very much further, in twentieth-century English horror and science fiction writing, in key works by William Hope Hodgson and Olaf Stapledon.

In Chapter 3, 'Seerman: the rise of the psychic detective', early detective fiction is noted (in particular, works by Schiller, Hoffmann and Poe), prior to an examination of the figure of the uncle in Odoevsky's *The Salamander* – this personage here being proposed as a proto-'psychic doctor' (of, at least, occultist erudition). Examples of such a figure, in Anglo-Irish and English literature up to the Edwardian era, are then considered. The discussion assesses works by Sheridan Le Fanu, Bram Stoker, Algernon Blackwood and, again, Hodgson. Such a protagonist is then seen to recede, in the main into a more parodic treatment. A concluding section notes the reappearance at least of such motifs (if not the exact figure) in recent 'metaphysical detective' fiction (as in works by Matthew Pearl and Julian Barnes).

In the last chapter, 'Monk: duelling confession within the novel', Odoevsky's (previously untranslated) story *The Witness* is seen as an important source for certain events in the autobiographical confession of the Elder Zosima in Dostoevsky's *The Brothers Karamazov* (or *The Karamazov Brothers*, as preferred by OUP). This has been briefly, but obscurely, noted before; unnoticed (to my knowledge), though, is a similar source, in Alessandro Manzoni's *The Betrothed*. These three works (or such key episodes there-from) contribute to a considerably wider ensuing discussion of the 'confessional' motif (when involving, in particular, duels and monks) in modern fiction, going back to the Gothic period and extending into the present century.

As an appendix (in its way perhaps serving as a second conclusion, in endwise emphasising the Odoevsky thread), I include two of his stories, translated here for the first time (representing too the 'Starman' and 'Monk' chapters).

The Odoevsky link apart (a still needed boost to his repu-tation, one might dare to hope), might there be any other elements to make these four chapters into something more of a whole, rather than a mere quartet of essays? Certainly, as compared with the much fuller comparative studies undertaken earlier or indeed my two books on Odoevsky,[3] the present project is rather more limited in scope and inten-tion. The four titular figures are therefore here being used towards an at least partial tracing of certain European literary developments, or 'pathways' into modern fiction.

Occasional touches of the absurd may appear. More prominent, certainly after the first chapter, are features frequently associated with the fantastic (involving the thriller and the occult, to name but two), plus a number of other recurring figures or texts.

Dostoevsky, as will already be apparent, is an important figure in two of the chapters (as indeed is Hoffmann, albeit to a slightly lesser extent, as well as Hodgson), but he also makes fleeting appearances elsewhere, under music and seer. He might also be a 'seer' in other senses as well; commonly regarded as a 'prophet', he was acclaimed, in a famous study of 1902 by the decadent writer D.S. Merezhkovsky, as 'the "seer" of a transcendental spiritual world, whose works were prophetic and revelatory in that they penetrated "the illusoriness of the real"'.[4] The French decadent, J.-K. Huysmans (or at least his protagonist Durtal), in 1891, for that matter, looking for 'the Spiritual Naturalism' of 'the regions above and beyond', had regarded Dostoevsky as the closest approximation, while commenting: 'Yet even that amenable Russian is more an evangelical socialist than an enraptured realist'.[5]

Chekhov appears here several times. His only Gothic-occult story, *The Black Monk* (1894), features briefly in the fourth chapter, as may be expected under 'monk'; but it contrives to earn a mention in the music category as well (and impinges briefly on the science fiction too, with its monkish flight pattern through time and outer space). Moreover, given that this story's main theme would appear to be madness, and that it is thought to have been influenced in part by a yet further Odoevsky story, *The Sylph* (a work included in Odoevsky, *The Salamander and Other Gothic Tales*), it could have featured prominently in a hypothetical fifth chapter centred on the 'madman'.[6] To cite Huysmans again (2001, 178), 'the only people who are worth knowing are either saints, scoundrels or madmen'. Or, to cite Andrei Leverkühn's devil: 'The artist is the brother of the criminal and the madman' (*DF*, 229).[7] However, this particular theme as a whole has probably been adequately enough covered elsewhere. A recent essay has linked Odoevsky's little-known character Segeliel' (who features both in a fragmentary novel of the 1830s and in the *Russian Nights* story 'The Improvisor') with Dostoevsky's Prince Myshkin (of *The Idiot*).[8] Two further aspects again of Odoevsky's fiction, barely mentioned here in passing, and contrasting considerably with his better-known Gothic-fantastic approaches, are his stories for children and his contributions to the subgenre of the 'society tale'.[9] However, these would perhaps not fit too comfortably with the strains of literary development investigated here, so four pathways may be a sufficient number for present purposes.

Other writers, or works, threatening to infiltrate almost anywhere in this study include Thomas Mann (with *The Magic Mountain*; *Doctor Faustus*; and *Confessions of Felix Krull, Confidence Man*) and Umberto Eco (*The Name of the Rose* and *Foucault's Pendulum* – not to mention his non-fictional and theoretical writings). Huysmans, at a later stage of the proceedings, as perhaps is already obvious, began to make similar incursions. Nabokov, Daniil Kharms and Orhan Pamuk make brief intrusions. Even Boris Akunin's *Pelagia & The Black Monk*, with its overt play on Chekhov's figure, as well as on works by Dostoevsky, could encroach too on detection (though employing a non-psychic conventual sleuth) and on at least elements towards science fiction. Moreover, Akunin even casts a nod at Odoevsky – if only as the (unnamed) writer of ever-popular children's fiction, by alluding to his story 'The Little Town in the Snuffbox'.

A writer recently coming to my notice, who might also conceivably have made an appearance here, is C.J. Sansom, with his Shardlake (to date) tetralogy: *Dissolution*, *Dark Fire*, *Sovereign* and *Revelation* (2003–8). However, while many of his Tudor monks do confess, they are not noted for their duelling exploits. And, moreover, although witchcraft and devilry are often floated as a smokescreen, the detection eventually required of Shardlake is not psychic. 'Does he too feel the devil in this?', one character asks. 'It is not a speculation that can profit us', comes the sharp reply. 'Possession', another laughs cynically: 'Is that what you think? That idea will get you nowhere'.[10] And neither does it.

Notes

1 Charles E. Passage, *The Russian Hoffmanists*, The Hague: Mouton, 1963.
2 V.F. Odoyevsky, *Romanticheskiye povesti*, intro. and selected bibliography by Neil Cornwell, repr. of 1929 Leningrad edn, Oxford: Willem A. Meeuws, 1975.
3 Neil Cornwell, *The Literary Fantastic*, Brighton: Harvester, 1990; *The Absurd in Literature*, Manchester: Manchester University Press, 2006; *The Life, Times and Milieu of V.F. Odoyevsky* (foreword by Sir Isaiah Berlin), London: The Athlone Press, and Athens, OH: Ohio University Press, 1986; *Vladimir Odoevsky and Romantic Poetics*, Providence and Oxford: Berghahn Books, 1998.
4 W.J. Leatherbarrow, *Fyodor Dostoyevsky: The Brothers Karamazov*, Cambridge: Cambridge University Press, 1992, p. 101.
5 Joris-Karl Huysmans, *The Damned [Là-Bas]*, trans. Terry Hale, London: Penguin, 2001, p. 6.
6 See on this Ann Komaromi, 'Unknown Force: Gothic Realism in Chekhov's *The Black Monk*', in Neil Cornwell, ed., *The Gothic-Fantastic in Nineteenth-Century Russian Literature*, Amsterdam and Atlanta, GA: Rodopi, 1999, pp. 257–75; and, summarising the Odoevsky angle, Claire Whitehead, 'Anton Chekhov's *The Black Monk*: An Example of the Fantastic?', *The Slavonic and East European Review*, 85, 4, Oct. 2007, pp. 601–28.
7 Thomas Mann, *Doctor Faustus*, trans. H.T. Lowe-Porter, Harmondsworth: Penguin, [1949] 1968, p. 229. Hereafter *DF*.
8 A.V. Koren'kov, 'Paralleli romana F.M. Dostoevskogo "Idiot" i misterii V.F. Odoevskogo "Segeliel'"', in *Dostojevskij a dnešok* (ed. Natália Muránska], Nitra, 2007, pp. 201–16.

9 The main examples in this latter mode are the novellas *Princess Mimi* and *Princess Zizi*: see Vladimir Odoevsky, *Two Princesses*, trans. Neil Cornwell, London: Hesperus, 2010. See also the collection *The Society Tale in Russian Literature: from Odoevskii to Tolstoi*, ed. Neil Cornwell, Amsterdam and Atlanta, GA: Rodopi, 1998.

10 C.J. Sansom, *Revelation*, Macmillan: London, 2008, pp. 280, 328.

1

Musicman: the musical-artistic story from Hoffmann and Odoevsky to Pasternak

The artistic story is an acknowledged subgenre of Romantic fiction. The 'artist' – usually a poet or writer, sometimes a painter, or occasionally a representative of another art form – is a common enough figure in Romantic literature, with extensions into the Gothic-fantastic, through the nineteenth and twentieth centuries. One has only to think of Bulgakov's 'Master' (in his celebrated *The Master and Margarita*). In other, on the whole more mainstream – though often at least equally complex – areas of, for instance, Russian fiction, another obvious figure of some prominence would be Doctor Iurii Zhivago. American campus fiction (without my wishing to reduce *Pale Fire* to that rather bland category) offers Vladimir Nabokov's rival figure of the poet, John Shade.

In the case of the art (painter or painting) story, we can trace a line from E.T.A. Hoffmann (in *Signor Formica* and *The Jesuit Chapel in G.*) through such following Romantics or romantic-realists as Gogol and Balzac. This would continue on, through Poe, Hawthorne, Wilde and Henry James, to the early Nabokov of *La Veneziana* (*Venetsianka*; written 1924, published posthumously), and of course beyond, into the present century. 'Portraits in words and portraits in paint are opposites, rather than metaphors for each other', in the view of A.S. Byatt.[1] Twentieth-century art novels seriously concerned with paintings, actual or fictional, include Dmitri Merezhkovsky's *The Romance of Leonardo da Vinci* (1902) and Salman Rushdie's *The Moor's Last Sigh*, to name just two.[2] More recently, too, we have Sarah Dunant's *The Birth of Venus* (2003). The composition of prose fiction primarily concerned with the actual painting of pictures (portraits or otherwise) may be a somewhat different matter; however, anything resembling a detailed analysis of the complexities and possible subdivisions of the artistic tale will have to remain outside the scope of the present chapter.

The musical story may seem, at first sight at least, a poor relation within the overall Romantic or neo-Romantic 'artistic' tradition, although two of Pushkin's dramatic 'Little Tragedies' had musical themes. Music makes its appearances too in Russian Romantic poetry and thought. Just five years after Odoevsky's *Russian Nights*, Dostoevsky produced what was to have been his first full-length novel, *Netochka Nezvanova* (1849), the first section of which is effectively a musical story, recounting the 'career' of the mad violinist Efim (stepfather of the eponymous narrator). The figure of Prince X may even have been based on (Prince) Odoevsky. Later parts, too, might have aspired to something of a musical path, given that Netochka subsequently proves to have a fine singing voice.

Moreover, such significant later works as *The Kreutzer Sonata* (*Kreitserova sonata*) by Tolstoy and (much later) Thomas Mann's *Doctor Faustus* (which has itself been analysed alongside *Doctor Zhivago*)[3] can also be invoked. Russian literature, it may here be stressed, provides – in addition to Tolstoy's novella of musically inspired jealousy, and the two main works to be discussed in the present chapter – a number of diverse offerings in prose fictional forms. These include: Korolenko's 'The Blind Musician' (*Slepoi muzykant*); Chekhov's 'Rothschild's Violin' (*Skripka Rotshil'da*); the so-called 'Symphonies' of Andrei Bely; Elena Guro's 'Picasso's Violin' (*Skripka Pikasso*); Nikolai Gumilev's 'The Stradivar-ius' (*Skripka Stradivariusa*), which invokes Paganini; and

'Moscow Violin' (*Moskovskaia skripka*) by Platonov (in which, it is argued, 'the main hero . . . appears to be the violin itself').[4] There are also later composer-based stories by Iurii Nagibin. Yet another violin is to be found, too, within the *oeuvre* of Pasternak: the poem *Skripka Paganini* (from *Poverkh bar'erov*).[5] An entertaining exercise, perhaps, would be to contrast Tolstoy's heavily moralistic *Kreutzer Sonata* with Chekhov's near-contemporaneous 'Romance with Double Bass' (*Roman s kontrabasom*), in which the double bass case owned by one Pitzikatoff is employed in the carrying around of a naked woman. It should be mentioned that English literature had also offered its own violin (indeed Stradivarius) novel, *The Lost Stradivarius* by John Meade Falkner (1895) – a work fusing its musical theme with the ghostly supernatural.

A perhaps at first sight unlikely Chekhov story, *The Black Monk* (*Chernyi monakh*) has not just 'the cyclic form that is typical of Chekhov's mature prose', but, as first pointed out by no less a figure than Shostakovich, it is a story built around a musical piece (Gaetano Braga's *Wallachian Legend* serenade), as well as being 'constructed in perfect and appropriate sonata form'.[6] *The Black Monk* has also been made into an opera, by the French composer Philippe Hersant (first performed 2005), from which he later arranged for piano the recital piece *In Black* (2009). Shostakovich also saw Chekhov's story *Gusev* (1890: not a musical story, but an account of a death at sea) as the most musical of Russian prose.[7] For that matter, too, a seemingly unpromising author, Nabokov – given his supposed lack of musical appreciation, as thought to be evidenced in his slightly later story 'Music' (*Muzyka*) – wrote another early story about an eponymous deranged pianist of 'deep and demented music', and composer of fugues, whom he called 'Bachmann' (*Bakhman*).[8] Nabokov is clearly by no means the only author mentioned here who will have been well aware of the rich possible analogies between the composition of music and prose. Thomas Mann, indeed (notwithstanding his having been something of a *bête noire* of Nabokov's) develops a 'tendency to musical prose' on the part of his fictional composer, Adrian Leverkühn (*DF*, 438).[9] Indeed, the 'artistic story' is perhaps inevitably engaged in the exploitation of connections between the arts. 'Art and prayer', for Huysmans at least, 'are the only pure ejaculations of the soul!'[10]

*   *   *   *   *

The European tradition of the musical story would appear to commence with Diderot. His novella *Rameau's Nephew* (*Le Neveu de Rameau*) was begun in 1761, though not published until 1823 (other than for a German translation by Goethe, in 1805). Before coming to the vital contribution made to this budding minor genre by Hoffmann, we should note Wackenroder's *Fantasies on Art* (or *Confessions and Fantasies*), completed, and again posthumously published, by Tieck in 1799, which includes the novella of the fictional musician Joseph Berglinger and his purported associated writings. Tieck's collection *Phantasus* (of 1812) also includes musical discussion. Another important early work was Kleist's story, significantly enough entitled *St Cecilia or the Power of Music* (of 1810–11).

In 1809, however, Hoffmann had launched his literary career with the tale *Ritter Gluck* (subtitled 'A Recollection from the Year 1809'), in which a mysterious and musically gifted gentleman claims to be the composer Gluck – who had in fact died twenty-two years earlier. This particular work would appear to have inspired Vladimir Odoevsky's artistic story, albeit dealing in another art medium, 'Opere del Cavaliere Giambattista Piranesi', in which a very similar situation arises. This brief work was published as an independent story in 1831, and later revised for incorporation into the philosophical frame-tale novel *Russian Nights* (*Russkie nochi*, 1844). As we shall see, Odoevsky also followed Hoffmann (and, for that matter, Diderot – while Pushkin's *Mozart and Salieri* should certainly not be forgotten either, not least as the original for Peter Shaffer's *Amadeus*) in composing literary works dealing with actual composers.

Hoffmann, who was of course a talented composer in his own right (some, at least, of whose works have been revived in recent times),[11] and an important music critic, left a considerable body of musical writings. These are both fictional and non-fictional – including some, indeed, which are hard to differentiate in this regard. We should mention at least two musical stories: *Don Juan* (of 1812; translated, appropriately enough, as it offers a fascinating treatment of the Mozart opera of that name, as *Don Giovanni*); and *Rat Krespel* (1818; known in English both as 'Councillor Krespel' and as 'The Cremona Violin'). More substantial, in respect of length, is the series (or cycle, conceived as a '*Musikalischer Roman*': Hoffmann 1989, 51; hereafter *HMW*), *Kreisleriana* (of 1814), which combines fiction with music criticism (and inspired a composition by Schumann, in another reversal of the trend discussed here – without mentioning the range of further musical adaptations from Hoffmann's tales); and the novel, with which it has apparent connections: *Kater Murr* (1819–21; translated as *The Life and Opinions of the Tomcat Murr*). The latter work may be considered a major, if eccentric, innovative novel of the nineteenth century: one which contrives to splice together the biography of the eccentric musician Johannes Kreisler – a Hoffmann *alter ego* – and the memoirs of the eponymous tomcat, Murr. Hoffmann designates instrumental music 'the most Romantic of all the arts' (*HMW*, 96) and his musical stories bring together Romanticist associations with madness and/or death – as well as heightened feelings of the sublime produced by music, and notions of synaesthesia, symbols and hieroglyphs.

Vladimir Odoevsky wrote, we may consider for present purposes at least, four 'artistic stories'. The first of these, 'Beethoven's Last Quartet' (*Poslednii kvartet Betkhovena*), appeared in 1830, and was followed a year later by the Piranesi story. A near-contemporary leading representative of Romantic (verging in his later work on a modernistic) experimentalism, greatly admired in Hoffmann's writings (Beethoven), thus sits alongside an artistic figure of the previous century (Piranesi), who, with his boundless neo-classical architectural designs, had been an archetypal inspiration to many of the Romantics. This was followed in 1833 by the story of 'The Improviser' (or 'Improvvisatore': *Improvizator*), in which a young poet obtains what is in effect diabolical assistance in the effortless composition of verse; and in 1835 came the longer 'biographical' tale of *Sebastian Bach* (*Sebastiian Bakh*). Each of these works was published as a separate story; but all were intended to form part of a grandiose portmanteau work, significantly to be entitled *The House of Madmen*, and all were eventually placed within its successor, *Russian Nights* (Odoevsky, 1997; hereafter *RN*). Links between these stories do suggest themselves, in their explorations of the nature of artistic feeling and the relation-ship of the artist to those around him. The sterile, mecha-nistic vision of Kipriano (the improviser who acquired creative ability illicitly from without rather than legitimately from within) may be set alongside the exhausted imagina-tion of the dying Bach. Bach then perceives, instead of exalted musical sounds, 'only the keys, the pipes, the valves of the organ' (*RN*, 189 / 132).[12] Something of the ambitious and largely unrealised (except for *Russian Nights*) literary edifices conceived by Odoevsky himself may be reflected in the anguish of his Piranesi and perhaps too in the last days of the deaf and misunderstood genius, Beethoven.[13]

*   *   *   *   *

We shall return shortly to Hoffmann – and in particular to Odoevsky, and also indeed to Bach. However, we should first begin to consider the phenomenon of the artistic story in relation to Pasternak. The artistic background in the Paster-nak family is extremely well known: music (his mother) blended with painting (his father) and various literary visi-tors. One memorable home concert presented a piano trio (probably one by Tchaikovsky) played before a distinguished audience which included, he claimed in *People and Proposi-tions* (*Liudi i polozheniia*, or 'An Autobiographical Essay', written in 1956; hereafter *PP*), the painter Nikolai Gei and Lev Tolstoy. That night stood out as 'a landmark and divid-ing line between the oblivion of infancy and my later child-hood' (*PP*, 30; *SS*, 4, 299). Subsequent meetings occurred with such figures as Rilke and Gorky – and, in particular, Skriabin (Alexander Scriabin).

If Pasternak's emergence in literature may be said (as by Christopher Barnes, with particular regard to the early poetry and polemical essays) to have taken place 'under the aegis of Futuristic innovation',[14] the first phase of his prose fiction may equally be described as 'post-Symbolist', 'early modernist' or 'neo-Romantic'. Conceivably the last phrase best fits his three 'artistic stories' of the period 1915 to 1918. The first and the third of these, *Apellesova cherta* ('The Apelles Mark') and *Pis'ma iz Tuly* ('Letters from Tula'), use poets as protagonists, with the first displaying an obvious debt to German Romantic literature through its employment of the name Heinrich Heine. The middle story, unfinished, or (the second half of it, at least) certainly unpolished, represents – as its title suggests – Pasternak's contribution to the tradi-tion, or the subgenre, of the musical story.

Istoriia odnoi kontroktavy, written in the winter holidays of 1916–17 (not in 1913, as had earlier been thought) and rediscovered only in 1960, was not published until the 1970s.[15] Christopher Barnes translated this work in 1986, in the first of his two volumes – Boris Pasternak, *The Voice of Prose* – under the title *Suboctave Story* (*VP*, 1, 129–56). While, it may be supposed, few would wish to rank this hastily written and apparently incomplete tale, which seems to have survived at all only by chance, among the most successful of Pasternak's achievements in prose, it is cer-tainly not without its points of interest – particularly in its first half.[16] For a summary of the story, we can do little better, probably, than to synthesise the synopses provided by Barnes:

> The story tells of a nineteenth-century provincial town organist in Germany, named Knauer. During his improvisations he is described surrendering totally to the controlling forces of inspiration, and during one such fantasia he fails to notice that his young son has clambered inside the organ chamber. As his father plays, the boy is crushed to death in the suboctave coupler mechanism (a highly unlikely occurrence, particularly in those days of hand-blown bellows and tracker action!). The solid local bourgeois citizens see the tragedy as the vengeance of Providence on the musician for his godless cult of art. Later, as he sits by the corpse of his son, the awful power of music dawns on Knauer too when he observes that his fingers are moving in octaves over the boy's body. Almost immediately the guilt-ridden musician flees the town. The story's conclusion is set ten years later [to be exact, in 1820, when Hoffmann was publishing the first volume of his *Kater Murr*: NC]. Knauer reappears, secretly tries out the organ, and applies to be reinstated. He is turned down. His application is a shameless act, the town council tells him, and his presence cannot be tolerated after he has again tampered with an instrument that he should never have dared to touch. Thereupon Knauer makes a second and final ignominious departure.[17]

Clearly an example of what Barnes calls Pasternak's 'aesthetic prose' (*VP*, 1, 2), or Larissa Rudova his 'pictorial prose' (Rudova, 1994, 7), and using impressionistic natural (at times animal) imagery, *Suboctave Story* treats the relationship between the artist and the elemental forces of art and nature – able to wield power over life and death. It was one of the works, like *Okhrannaia gramota* itself (*A Safe Conduct*, written a decade or so later), according to Pasternak in his 'Autobiographical Essay', composed – or indeed, he insisted, 'spoilt' – by 'unnecessary affectation' (*nenuzhnaia manernost'*), 'the besetting sin of that period' (*PP*, 26; *SS*, 4, 296).

As its setting might indicate, and as commentators have demonstrated since its first full publication, *Subocatve Story* owes its inspiration first to elements of German Romanticism (overtly suggested by the period and location of its action) and secondly to Pasternak's own German experiences. These, as we know, date from his stays in Berlin in 1906 and Marburg in 1912. And the first of the two sojourns would seem to have particular relevance for the present tale. Alexander Pasternak's memoirs vividly record the visits of the two Pasternak brothers to Philharmonia concerts and, on Berlin Sundays, 'to the nearby Gedächtniskirche', where the 'acoustics, organist and organ were excellent'; weekday visits were made also to hear 'the organist practising, and trying out different interpretations of Bach's melodies' (Pasternak, 1984, 134). He was at his best at the end of the services, as the church emptied, when, as Alexander expatiates:

> Heated by his appeal to the Almighty, Bach seemed to cry out, obstinate and insistent, thrusting aside the walls as a deep breath distends the rib-cage. Sound intensified on sound, super-charging the atmosphere, till we lost all bodily sense. Everything, it seemed, was lost in a vast universe – and yet we were held tight in a powerful grasp, the deep supporting boom of the bass. The last, superhuman chords sounded. The organ fell silent, attentive to the answering echo cast by the church's newly resurrected windows, walls and vaults. Drained of sensation, and wondering that the streets and houses should still be standing, we were the last to leave, silently, for home. (ibid.)

The organ and Bach (stressed together by Alexander) are the important things to note here, as well, of course, as the ecstatic emotion occasioned by the music and by the dedication and the artistry of the performance. This certainly sounds but a small step from the *Suboctave Story* – one of the early prose tales composed by his brother, as Alexander himself puts it, 'in the perpetually restless style of pure German Romanticism' (ibid. 139). Music was vitally important to Pasternak; 'already a Wagner enthusiast', he frequented Berlin performances of the symphonic poems of Richard Strauss and 'the symphonies and concerti of Beethoven and Brahms' (Barnes, 1989, 1, 66).

Before returning to Germany, six years later, to undertake philosophical studies at Marburg, Boris had, as we may know, finally rejected a musical career. Similarly, he was later to repudiate the Romantic style of writing (together with the Romantic idea of the life of the artist) – 'characteristically' (as Alexander saw it), 'as though it had never influenced him at all' (ibid.).

In a letter from Marburg to his student friend Konstantin Loks, Pasternak had written of the historical-artistic ambience pervading that town as possessed of 'a dark and imperious predisposition – for the organ, for the Gothic, for something torn out and uncompleted that is buried here' (*SS*, 4, 861; *SS*, 5, 36). A few years later, very soon after writing – though never quite completing – his *Suboctave Story*, Pasternak wrote from the Urals to Loks. Referring to the almost suicidal condition in which 'I once threw up music', he – now in particular, it seems (in late January 1917) – sees this move as 'a direct act of amputation, cutting off the most vital part of my existence'. 'I have killed in myself the main thing', Pasternak continues:

> I only have to pour out all that is boiling up inside me in some improvisation unlit by paraffin, and the burning need for a *composer's biography* begins to visit me like a shaken harmony, like a disaster that has befallen me, persistently and inescapably like an *elemental claim*. [Pasternak's emphasis] (Barnes, 1977, 317; *SS*, 5, 99)

The abandoning of music, nearly eight years before, had obviously affected Pasternak deeply, and some of this feeling, clearly, is subsumed into *Suboctave Story*. At the same time, like certain of his other repudiations, Pasternak's rejection of music should not be seen as absolutely total. Barnes (1977, 320) has pointed out that 'Pasternak's verse abounds in musical references and terminology'. Musically analogous forms of construction have been discerned, too, within the poetics of Pasternak's later prose.[18]

Beethoven was clearly a figure of some importance for Pasternak, beyond the attendance of a few Berlin concerts. He drafted an early poem, at first called 'Sounds of Beethoven in the Street' (*Zvuki Betkhovena v ulitse*), and subsequently something more like 'Beethoven of the Sidewalks' (*Betkhoven mostovykh*), again published only some years after his death. This includes the couplet: 'And suddenly Beethoven hauls / Sonatas' shackles on the square' (*SS*, 1, 580; trans. Barnes, 1989, 1, 113), and the manuscript had been given by Pasternak to Loks in 1912 (*SS*, 1, 737). At the beginning of 1916 Pasternak asked his parents to send him the scores of works by Beethoven (along with Mozart, Schubert and Wagner: Barnes, 1989, 1, 200) and in the early 1920s Dmitrii Petrovsky thought fit to dedicate his poem 'Beethoven' to Pasternak.

What Barnes (1977, 320) terms Pasternak's 'lifelong appreciation and understanding of the art of music', however, is much later given its head in the essay he published in 1945 on 'Chopin'.[19] In this piece (written for the 135th anniversary of Chopin's birth) he conjures with 'the meaning of realism in music' (*PP*, 274; *SS*, 4, 403). Whatever exactly might be made of that vexed topic, Pasternak identifies as two 'exceptions to the exceptions', Bach and Chopin. These 'mainstays and creators of instrumental music' he sees as 'personifications of undisguised authenticity'. 'Their music', for Pasternak, 'abounds in detail and gives the impression of *a chronicle of their lives*. In their *works*, more than anyone else's, actual reality emerges forth from the sound' (ibid.) [emphases mine]. Once again, we may choose to see it as significant that Bach should be named in such a context.

A plethora of Romantic ideas can be seen reflected in *Suboctave Story*. Schelling held that the work of art 'must be a perfect microcosm of all creation, just as the cosmos at large constitutes a vast work of art' (Cardinal, 1975, 83). The arts are therefore interconnected; many artistic figures, or creators, span more than one art form (and Tieck, for instance, could produce 'verbal music': *HMW*, 68). Literature, Rudova stresses (1994, 53), is treated by Pasternak (right up to his description of Zhivago's creative process) as 'a syncretic art'; indebted to Romantic aesthetics, this notion of 'inspiration', shared too by Rilke, is filtered through the Symbolists' aspirations to create synthetic works of art. Friedrich Schlegel applied a notion of 'permanent incompleteness' to Romantic poetry (see *HMW*, 61, n. 86), and Romantic advocacy of the fragment as form may harmonise with the non-completion of many a Romantic and neo-Romantic work – including perhaps the *Suboctave Story*.

One should not forget the impact on Pasternak, over a number of years, of the personality and the artistic power of Skriabin (his music and his Nietzscheanism). The more powerful the spell cast by Skriabin himself, Pasternak relates in *Safe Conduct*, 'the more it shielded me from the ravages wrought by his indescribable music' (*VP*, 23; *SS*, 4, 151). And music can bring ravages; the conjuring of inspiration into signs and symbols, Hoffmann's Kreisler warns, can result in 'the demonic misuse of music' – even though it may be followed by 'the ascent to higher things and . . . transfiguration through music and song!' (*HMW*, 165). Music, for Hoffmann, 'is a form of religious worship' (*HMW*, 355) and real (or modern) music was 'first revealed in Italy when Christianity shone forth in its greatest splendour' (*HMW*, 356). It is probably not accidental, therefore, that music should be particularly associated with the organ and a (Lutheran) church setting in the works here under consideration (albeit, and perhaps significantly, at times referred to as 'temple': *khram*). 'The great masters', moreover, 'live on in spirit', writes Hoffmann, concluding his essay on 'Old and New Church Music' (*HMW*, 376). A number of these notions can be seen as still exercising Pasternak's consciousness in *Safe Conduct*. This is not least the case in the third section of Part One, where Conservatoire rehearsals for Skriabin's *Poem of Ecstasy* are described in a quintessential poetical and atmospheric prose. The music itself is prefaced by the employment of animal imagery (though of a circus variety, and not quite in the vein of *Kater Murr*): 'Like an animal driven back with staves into its winter area, the music kept slapping a paw up on to the wooden casing of the organ' (*VP*, 25; *SS*, 4, 153). Wagner, Van Gogh and Chopin are then invoked within a few lines. 'I loved music more than anything in the world' – Pasternak continues – 'and Scriabin more than anyone in music'; however, music for Pasternak was 'a cult – that is the destructive point where all my most superstitious, self-abnegating elements focused' (*VP*, 26; *SS*, 4, 154). Once again, we encounter the potentially dangerous effect of music.

A number of Romantic pre-texts of relevance to *Suboctave Story* have been suggested, as has the presence of several intermediate texts. Kleist's *St Cecilia or the Power of Music* is mentioned: by Barnes (*VP*, 11), by Daša di Simplicio (1990, 102) and by Karen Evans-Romaine (1997, 11–12), who cites too a 1973 dissertation by Erika Freiberger Sheikholeslami. In this story, four iconoclast brothers are dispatched into a witless religious trance, broken only when they howl a *Gloria in excelsis* like leopards and wolves, by the performance of an Italian mass, apparently conducted from the organ by a ghostly apparition of the eponymous saint herself. Hoffmann, not surprisingly, has been mentioned in this connection by commentators from E.B. Pasternak and Alexander Pasternak onwards. Evans-Romaine (1997, 250) introduces discussion too of Heine's motif of the broken string.

Evans-Romaine (ibid., 171) notes that 'the presence of Hoffmann subtexts in Pasternak's work often shows the overlay of contemporary writers who also read Hoffmann'. Among such modernist (or neo-Romantic) texts, suggestions have been put forward with reference to Hauptmann's *Michael Kramer* (strongly recommended to Russians in 1900 by Rilke – see Di Simplicio, 1990, 101); works by the Polish decadent Stanisław Przybyszewski (evoked by Pasternak in his late 'Autobiographical Essay' – see Evans-Romaine, 1997, 210). Furthermore (also noted by Evans-Romaine), there is Andrei Bely's little-read essay 'Protiv muzyky' ('Against Music' of 1907). In his *Suboctave Story*, she considers, 'Pasternak realizes the metaphor of Belyj's essay' in a tale which 'portrays between the lines the mediocrity and falsehood, as well as the destructive power, of the self-absorbed artist' (ibid., 223).

*   *   *   *   *

Let us return now to Hoffmann and to Odoevsky. Evans-Romaine (ibid., 174–83) sees *Ritter Gluck* as a subtext to four early Pasternak texts (plus a letter), while noting that Anna Ljunggren too had written of Hoffmann's impact on Pasternak's earliest prose texts (Ljunggren, 1984, 124–6). More particularly, though, Evans-Romaine regards *The Life and Opinions of Kater Murr* as the important subtext to *Suboctave Story*.[20] The death of Knauer's son she sees as 'a much darker version' of a scene in *Kater Murr* (Evans-Romaine, 1997, 217). This occurs when the organ builder and music teacher Abraham Liscov playfully (as he thinks) pulls the footstool from under the feet of his pupil, the young Kreisler, and then takes a hammer to the spinet, the instrument he has been called in to repair (*KM*, 85–6). The same commentator also sees the name 'Knauer' in Pasternak's story as deriving from the characterisations of the boy in this 'key scene' – **Kna**be (boy) and his name, Kreisl**er** (Evans-Romaine, 1997, 219) – and notes a common theme of insanity. Knauer's first name, Amadeus, we might add, is also a genuflection to Hoffmann (who had himself adopted it in homage to Mozart). A number of moments of musical ecstasy occur in Hoffmann's novel. Liscov is said to have 'mad fancies and wild ideas' and the young Kreisler's interest in him 'grew to the utmost awe and admiration when he first heard the mighty tones of the beautiful organ in the town's principal church' (*KM*, 84).[21] Liscov subsequently 'saw the boy . . . hammering out Sebastian Bach's most difficult sonatas with a proud air and an almost adult touch' (*KM*, 197). The grown up Kreisler has 'a profound sense of being good for nothing in a world which seems to me an eternal and mysterious kind of dissonance' (*KM*, 217).

There is clearly much in *Kater Murr* that might have contributed towards Pasternak's composition of his *Suboctave Story*. However, the key subtext – or in particular the key anticipatory scene for Part One of *Suboctave Story* – is surely one contained within Odoevsky's *Sebastian Bach*. The scene in question has already been noticed in a footnote by Erika Greber (1989, 230–1, n. 91), though not developed – her main concern being with the Improviser, also of Odoevsky's *Russian Nights*, in connection with the improvisatory episode in Pasternak's *Povest'* (known in English as *Seryozha's Story*, or as *The Last Summer*). *Russian Nights* (as Greber notes: ibid.) had been reprinted in 1913, indeed for the first time since 1844, and this event gave rise to a modest renewal of critical interest in Odoevsky. We can assume that this development went not unnoticed by Pasternak. We can also assume, from the foregoing, that stories of artistic biography – and, in particular, one featuring a church, an organ and the figure of Johann Sebastian Bach – could not but have struck a special chord with Pasternak at this stage in his artistic evolution. While she does not name Odoevsky among her examples, Evans-Romaine (1997, 288) argues that 'the role of nineteenth-century Russian writers, primarily Romantics, as intermediaries in Pasternak's reception of the German Romantics . . . deserves greater attention'.

Hoffmann regarded Mozart and Haydn as the creators of modern instrumental music, with Beethoven unveiling before us 'the realm of the mighty and the immeasurable' (*HMW*, 97). 'How pale and insignificant everything seems', writes Hoffmann-Kreisler, 'that does not come from

[Beethoven], from the intelligence of Mozart, or from the mighty genius of Sebastian Bach' (ibid., 100). Hoffmann stresses that 'Bach's music bears the same relationship to that of the early Italians as the cathedral in Strasbourg to St Peter's in Rome' (ibid., 104). It is by his 'splendid old friend Sebastian' that Hoffmann feels himself 'borne high into the air on powerful wings' (ibid., 457). And, for both Hoffmann and Pasternak, Evans-Romaine (1997, 205) has noted, 'the authenticity of the music of Bach lies in its lack of affectation'.

For Odoevsky too, music was 'an art to express the inexpressible – that is to say that which can be expressed by no other means, other than by music itself' (see Cornwell, 1986, 134). A synthetic view of the arts must have been in his mind when he wrote of a suite by Bach: 'It's like walking in a gallery filled with Holbein and Dürer' (ibid., 133–4). Bach was always Odoevsky's 'most beloved composer' (*RN*, 1975, 291) and he did much to promote him in the St Petersburg of the 1830s, where (as elsewhere in Europe) he had fallen into total neglect. Late in life he was still setting himself 'to transpose a Bach chorale for organ and piano', while his own home-made organ was fondly named 'Sebastianon' (Cornwell, 1986, 148). Hoffmann's impact – both aesthetic and literary – on Odoevsky may be taken here as read: not entirely for no reason was he frequently dubbed 'the Russian Hoffmann'.[22] The musical connection was equally strong, forming a large part in their parallel careers: Hoffmann as writer, composer and legal functionary; Odoevsky as (among many other things) writer, music critic and government functionary – on which I have written in some detail elsewhere.[23]

In his Beethoven and Bach stories, Odoevsky, like Hoffmann before him, doubled in the role of writer and musicologist to construct sensitive, but highly imaginative, 'fictional biographies'. 'Beethoven's Last Quartet' begins with an epigraph from *Rat Krespel*, stressing alleged insanity. In the case of *Sebastian Bach*, realistic domestic details mingle with a largely invented account of the birth and fruition of artistic genius. In a discourse that reaches the reader of *Russian Nights* through several layers of narrative remove, Odoevsky presents what we may consider as two spokesmen for his own (Hoffmannian) Romantic aesthetics (or, at least, the Romantic systems with which he wishes to engage).[24] The first of these two is the eccentric 'investigator' and ostensible originator of the 'biography', who confides that there is 'only one source for the artist's life: his works' (*RN*, 157 / 106).[25] Furthermore, he claims, 'poets often answer each other like echoes among cliffs'; 'the Strasbourg bell tower is an adjunct to the Egyptian pyramids; Beethoven's symphonies are a second set of Mozart's symphonies' (*RN*, 155 / 103–4). Secondly, we have the young Sebastian's mentor – the master organ-builder Albrecht, doubling in the role of acting high priest of Romantic philosophy. Albrecht conducts supreme master classes in 'the perfection of the medium of this wonderful art' (*RN*, 176 / 121) – that is to say, the art of inspirational performance on the organ.

All this would, no doubt, have been of quite some interest to Pasternak, but the scene that must have impressed him most occurs when the young Sebastian is brought by his somewhat tyrannical elder brother Johann Christoph (acting *in loco parentis*) for Lutheran confirmation at a church in Eisenach. 'Here', we are told, 'Sebastian heard the sounds of an organ for the first time', as 'the full, overpowering harmony descended from Gothic vaults like the rush of a storm' (*RN*, 163 / 110). So overwhelmed is he by the mighty noise – and the awesome mechanics – of the organ that he steals back at night, 'to find out from where and how the enchanting sound that had taken possession of his soul this morning came' (*RN*, 165 / 111). Tired from his efforts to play this instrument, he climbs up a ladder into the organ. Here, in an exercise rich in Romantic defamiliarisation, Odoevsky presents Sebastian's nocturnal vision, as 'the mystery of architecture joined with the mysteries of harmony': 'variegated veils of contrasting sounds coiled and uncoiled in front of him, and a chromatic scale like a playful bas-relief rippled down the cornice' (*RN*, 166 / 113). Sebastian wakes up to daylight, still inside the organ. So shocked is Christoph by what he sees as his brother's feckless surrender to untrammelled emotion that he soon sinks into a mortal illness.[26] The organ at Eisenach, in all its sonorous and architectural majesty, has thus – indirectly at least – caused the demise of the father figure to the emerging artistic genius.

In Pasternak's version, the father is the rampant organist, carried away by his 'furious extemporizings' (*VP*, 133; *SS*, 4, 444). A boy, who has again crept into an organ, is this time physically slain by the mechanism of the instrument. The young Gottlieb, son of the organist Knauer, has climbed into the organ on which his father plays in what Erika Greber (1989, 230, n. 91) calls 'a genuine orgy of musical passion'; and this time, she says, 'the organ is a murder weapon, an organ of a destructive passion'. As she also points out, Albrecht warns Sebastian with regard to the organ: 'Only the soul immersed in a silent prayer gives a soul to its wooden pipes; and they, solemnly ringing through the air, display its own greatness before it' (*RN*, 179 / 123). It would seem to be this propensity of the organ that has been abused, or disregarded, by Pasternak's organist as, at the moment of catastrophe: 'The entire improvisation was suddenly dispossessed and orphaned' (*VP*, 130; *SS*, 4, 442). The 'inhuman shriek' (*nechelovecheskii krik* or *neob"iasnimyi vopl'*) that arose 'from behind the majestic rampart of pipes and ventils' (ibid.) may be related to 'the imprint of the first sinful wail' (*pechat' pervogo greshnogo voplia*), of which Sebastian is warned by Albrecht, with regard to the human singing voice (*RN*, 179 / 123). It also, we can now say, recalls what the young Boris perceived as 'actual cries for help and messages of disaster' that had come from the unfamiliar 'timbre of the stringed instruments' in the memorable home concert marking the end of his infancy (*PP*, 30; *SS*, 4, 299). Caressing 'in octaves' his son's corpse with his 'incorrigible hand', Knauer 'learned for the first time – learned for himself and not merely heard from others – that he had a soul' – though one 'in the maelstrom' of which he was now drowning (*VP*, 136–7; *SS*, 4, 448–9).

Part Two of *Suboctave Story* is unfinished, unpolished and – arguably – unsuccessful. 'So ends this story of a suboctave coupler on the organ', Pasternak writes; and this also marks 'the beginning of the tale of Knauer's ill-fame' (*VP*, 155; *SS*, 467). It may be over-ornate in its neo-Romantic nature imagery (especially in comparison with Odoevsky's generally more restrained and traditional Romantic prose style), and is certainly confusing to the first-time reader, not least on account of its adoption of an oblique narrative viewpoint. Nevertheless it does include something of what may be seen as a farcical parody of the events of Part One – through the agency of a moaning barrel-organ at a gypsy fair, together with monkeys, a camel and the demise of a she-bear.

Pasternak had dazzled and 'annihilated' his younger brother in Berlin with his use of musical terminology (repeated, one might say, at the beginning of *Suboctave Story*), especially by 'the strange slip of a word "continuo", that seemed to have slid from the organ of St Cecilia herself' (Pasternak, 1984, 132). 'Boris preferred to improvise', Alexander tells us, 'seeing himself as a future composer, not a performer' (ibid., 131). At the 'Serdarda' group, which Boris frequented, he admits that he 'used to do improvised piano portraits of each person as he arrived while the company was gathering at the start of the evening' (*PP*, 51; *SS*, 4, 318). In this 'Autobiographical Essay', Pasternak acknowledges, though, that he 'scorned whatever was not creative, or smacked of the artisan' (ibid., 37; 306). He thus 'avoided the exercises he detested' (Alexander emphasises), having 'no technical skill whatsoever, as he admits in *Safe Conduct*' (Pasternak, 1984, 131). 'I was hopeless as a practical performer', he reiterates himself in the later memoir (*PP*, 36; *SS*, 4, 305), so he would doubtless have appreciated Albrecht's verdict on the young Sebastian: 'You are not a craftsman. It is not your job to chisel keys: another, higher task is destined for you' (*RN*, 173 / 118). What weighed with Sebastian was a 'religious inspiration' (*RN*, 182 / 126) and a technical obsession with the art of the organ. Pasternak brings the organ into his revision of the poem 'Ballada' in 1928 (noted by Lazar Fleishman as 'bringing it close to the *fabula* of *Suboctave Story*': Fleishman, 1981, 104).

Odoevsky romanticises and 'Italianises' Sebastian's wife Magdalena (while incidentally rolling Bach's two wives into one) as a pretext for the injection of a Hoffmannesque conflict between German and Italian music. 'Lüneberg musicians', we are told, 'used to say of her that she resembled an Italian theme developed in the German manner' (*RN*, 174 / 119). This finds no immediate reflection in Pasternak's tale, but Pasternak's own susceptibility to Italian culture was succumbed to and nourished in the post-Marburg trip to Venice, finding vivid memoiristic and aesthetic reproduction in *Safe Conduct*. He never got to St Peter's in Rome, but he did manage to improvise on the image of the Venetian *pianta leone*. This produces citation of the Byronic 'Planter [or hoister] of the Lion', then goes from 'Pantaloon' to 'victorious Venice', continuing on to 'the haunting sight of lions' muzzles', and culminating in 'the leonine roar of an imaginary immortality' (*VP*, 75–6; *SS*, 4, 205–7).

*   *   *   *   *

To summarise and conclude, the following points may be stressed.

Hoffmann, Odoevsky and Pasternak were, all three, musicians (and, at least to a degree, composers). Each was eminently capable of writing convincingly on musical themes and compositional and instrumental technicalities – unlike other exponents of the musical story: its instigator Diderot, we are told, 'knew next to nothing about music' (Diderot, 1981, 26). And each brought fully Romantic dilations to bear on their musical fictions. Moreover, from known aspects of their lives, each interrogated certain autobiographical impulses, as well as bringing biographical aspects to their fictional musicmen.

Through their intense relations with music, we can now say, Odoevsky's Sebastian, Pasternak's Knauer and Pasternak himself (and very possibly Hoffmann and Skriabin too could be added to this list) killed something in or of themselves. The instances of Knauer and of Pasternak himself have already been spelt out. In the case of Odoevsky's Bach, he sacrificed all to his art, including 'family joys' (*RN*, 200 / 140), rejecting the Italian *canzonettas* beloved by his Magdalena (although the historical Bach, of course, *did* develop Italian themes!). By the end, 'half of his soul was dead' (*RN*, 189 / 131).

The destructive power of art, and of music in particular, is linked to death, and is liable to induce either perceived or actual insanity: such words as 'crank', 'eccentric' and 'madman' (or *chudak, original, sumasshedshii* – and *bezumie*) are commonly found in the musical story. Indeed, narratives of the 'mad musician' may in any case constitute a subcategory of the musical story (just as they may of the theme of madness). It was not purely accidental that his *vysokie bezumtsy* (or lofty madmen) – Beethoven, Bach, the improviser and the pseudo-Piranesi – had been intended by Odoevsky for the 'House of Madmen'. Similarly (indeed, strikingly so) to Odoevsky's Beethoven, Hoffmann had written of the initial 'failure' of Mozart's *Don Giovanni*: 'there were many who called the great composer a lunatic who could only write confusing rubbish that was without rhyme or reason and that nobody could play' (*HMW*, 440).

Albrecht had recounted to Sebastian a potted mythic history of humankind and the birth of art, using an imagery analogous to that found in Hoffmann's *Meister Floh*, and deriving from such Romantic thinkers as G.H. von Schubert, Oken and Carus. This provides, apart from anything else, the ironic spectacle of Bach, the towering genius of contrapuntal baroque and classical form, being raised on an ultra-Romantic philosophy. Again we can link this to Hoffmann, who, in his 'Review of Beethoven's Mass in C', could write of 'the pure romanticism living and moving in Mozart's and Haydn's fantastical compositions' (*HMW*, 328), while Mozart's 'Requiem' he described as 'truly romantic-sacred music, proceeding from his innermost soul' (ibid., 329). With such Romanticising of the classical repertoire in mind, it may not be quite such an impossible leap onward to Chopin, in the Berlin of 1924, when Alexander Pasternak remarks on his mother still playing 'Chopin études, his naggingly painful ballades and preludes' (Pasternak, 1984, 199). Or, indeed, to 1945, when Boris Pasternak can discern a chronicle of their lives within the works of Chopin and Bach (in Chopin's études he sees 'chapters of a pianoforte introduction to death')[27] – and therein an undoubtedly higher form of realism.

*   *   *   *   *

Purely as an epilogue, further brief reference will now be made to Mann's *Doctor Faustus: The Life of the German Composer Adrian Leverkühn as Told by a Friend* (original publication 1947), mentioned earlier just in passing. Pasternak and Mann were of course near contemporaries. Although the doctors Faustus–Zhivago parallel is not one to be pursued here (see, though, n. 3), we may just notice that the years in which Pasternak was pursuing his musical interests and preparing his *Suboctave Story* correspond to formative years in the development of Mann's protagonist, Leverkühn. Skriabin (who developed theosophical ideas and his own harmonic combinations) is – strangely perhaps – a composer not mentioned in *Doctor Faustus* (one of the few, one might say). Musically at least, Leverkühn is based on the perpetrator of the dodecaphonic scale, Arnold Schoenberg (again, not himself mentioned – at least until he is acknowledged in the 'Author's Note': *DF*, 491). In other respects (according to Elizabeth Butler) Leverkühn is drawn from the Urfaust-book, Dostoevsky's Ivan Karamazov, and elements of Nietzsche – combined into the creation of a mad musician.[28]

Sebastian Bach is mentioned more than a dozen times (including his organ music; and his 'pregnant polyphony': *DF*, 77; in addition he is occasionally played by Leverkühn: 111). Beethoven receives rather fuller discussion (e.g. 53–60) and is said to have 'been seen composing in words' (159). A lecture on 'Beethoven and the Fugue', and ensuing debate on Beethoven's abilities to write in the fugue form (57–60), surprisingly make no mention of the *Grosse Fuge*, Op. 133 (the work which probably inspired Odoevsky's story 'Beethoven's Last Quartet').[29]

Considerable description is given over to fictional music. Leverkühn's mature compositions include *The Revelation of St John* (the *Revelation* being a book of interest also to the later Zhivago-Pasternak) and the *Lamentation of Doctor Faustus* (Goethe's *Faust*, Part One, was translated by Pasternak in the early 1950s). Odoevsky had made free with his own idiosyncratic take on the figure of Faust in his *Russian Nights* (as well as a slightly strange *Faust* reference in his story *The Cosmorama* [*Kosmorama*, 1840]). Hoffmann, from whom Leverkühn and his mentors could have gained much of their insight into the black arts, was not averse to Kreislerian side-glances at Mephistopheles (*HMW*, 81, 136). In addition to establishing his mark in succession to Goethe, Mann was concerned too with European musical-artistic interpretations of Faust.[30] His fictional creation Leverkühn, at least, could thus purport to add himself, in an extremely modernistic manner, to the ranks of actual composers noted for their Faust compositions: Berlioz, Gounod, Liszt and Wagner in particular.

Notes

1 A.S. Byatt, *Portraits in Fiction*, London: Chatto & Windus, 2001, p. 1.

2 Byatt, noting the Rushdie novel, illustrates her comments with Bhupen Kharkar's portrait of that novelist himself: *Salman Rushdie: The Moor* (see Byatt, *Portraits in Fiction*, pp. 73–7).

3 See Henrik Birnbaum, *Doktor Faustus und Doktor Schiwago*, Lisse: Peter de Ridder Press, 1976.

4 David M. Bethea and Clint Walker, 'Platonov's Revisiting of Pushkin's Sculptural Myth: Notes for a Violin with Silent Orchestra', *Essays in Poetics*, 27, Autumn 2002, *A Hundred Years of Andrei Platonov: Platonov Special Issue in Two Volumes, Vol. II*, ed. Angela Livingstone, pp. 63–96 (p. 82).

5 Boris Pasternak, *Sobranie sochinenii v piati tomakh*, Moscow: Khudozhestvennaia literatura, 1989–92, vol. 1, pp. 472–4 (hereafter in the text as *SS*, followed by volume and page numbers).

6 Exposition and two themes, development and recapitulation: see Donald Rayfield, *Understanding Chekhov: A Critical Study of Chekhov's Prose and Drama*, London: Bristol Classical Press, 1999, p. 128. For an analysis, see Rosamund Bartlett, 'Sonata Form in Chekhov's *The Black Monk*', in Andrew Baruch Wachtel, ed., *Intersections and Transpositions: Russian Music, Literature and Society*, Evanston, IL: Northwestern University Press, 1998, pp. 58–72.

7 Philip Ross Bullock, 'Shostakovich and Literature', *The Literary Encyclopedia*, www.litencyc.com. The source for this observation is Elizabeth Wilson's memoir, *Shostakovich: A Life Remembered* [1994], London: Faber, 2006.

8 Vladimir Nabokov, *Collected Stories*, Harmondsworth: Penguin, 1997, pp. 116–24. On Nabokov and Bach, and the 'contrapuntal theme', see Gerard de Vries, 'Nabokov's *Pale Fire*, its structure and the last works of J.S. Bach', *Cycnos*, 24, 1, 2007, pp. 81–93. 'La Veneziana' and 'Bachmann' both date from 1924; 'Music' appeared in 1932. For more on Nabokov and music, see the introduction and several of the essays in Liza Zunshine, ed., *Nabokov at the Limits: Redrawing Critical Boundaries*, New York and London: Garland, 1999; and Yuri Leving,

'Singing *The Bells* and *The Covetous Knight*: Nabokov and Rachmaninoff's Operatic Translations of Poe and Pushkin', in Will Norman and Duncan White, eds, *Transitional Nabokov*, Oxford: Peter Lang, 2009, pp. 205–25.

9 ' "I have", Adrian said to me, "not wanted to write a sonata but a novel" ' (*DF*, 438).

10 Joris-Karl Huysmans, *The Damned (Là-Bas)*, trans. Terry Hale, Harmondsworth: Penguin, 2001, p. 196.

11 Hoffmann's opera *Undine* is available on CD on the Living Stage label (a live performance from 1966, remastered 1999: LS347.03 A-B).

12 Page numbers to Odoevsky (*RN*) relate to the English translation, followed by the 1975 'Literaturnye pamiatniki' edition.

13 Links have been established too between uncompleted works by Odoevsky of the 1820s and the artistic stories of the first half of the 1830s: see A.V. Koren'kov, 'Ot "Iordana Bruno . . ." k "Sebastiianu Bakhu" ', *Vestnik Rossiiskogo universiteta druzhby narodov*, seriia Literaturovedenie. Zhurnalistika, vol. 1, 1996, pp. 40–7.

14 Boris Pasternak, *The Voice of Prose, Volume One*, ed. Christopher Barnes, Edinburgh: Polygon, 1986, pp. 1, 8; hereafter *VP*.

15 The story first appeared in abridged form in *Izvestiia Akademiia nauk SSSR (Seriia literatury i iazyka)*, 1974, no. 2; and in complete form in *Slavica Hierosolymitana*, 1, 1977. Textual quotations and page numbers here are taken from *VP*, 1, followed by *SS*, 4 (pp. 440–68; and annotations, pp. 860–4).

16 Barnes variously describes this work as 'left as a half-finished manuscript' (*VP*, 1, 10) and 'never quite completed' (*VP*, 1, 257).

17 This account is conflated from *VP*, 1, 11; and Barnes, 1989, 220.

18 See, for instance, Boris Gasparov, 'Vremennoi kontrapunkt kak formoobrazuiushchii printsip romana Pasternaka "Doktor Zhivago" ', in Lazar Fleishman, ed., *Boris Pasternak and His Times: Selected Papers from the Second International Symposium on Pasternak*, Berkeley: Berkeley Slavic Specialties, 1989, pp. 315–58. English version in Wachtel, ed., *Intersections and Transpositions*.

19 *PP*, 274–8; Livingstone, *Pasternak on Art and Creativity*, 183–6; *SS* 4, 403–6.

20 E.T.A. Hoffmann, *The Life and Opinions of Tomcat Murr*, trans. Anthea Bell, 'Harmondsworth; Penguin, 1999; hereafter *KM*.

21 Quotations from *Kater Murr* are taken from the Penguin translation.

22 On Hoffmann and Odoevsky, see Charles E. Passage, *The Russian Hoffmannists*, The Hague: Mouton, 1963; Norman W. Ingham, *E.T.A. Hoffmann's Reception in Russia*, Würzburg: jal-Verlag, 1974; A.B. Botnikova, *E.T.A. Gofman i russkaia literatura*, Voronezh: Izd. Voronezhskogo un-ta, 1977. See also Slobodan Sucur, *Poe, Odoyevsky, and Purloined Letters: Questions of Theory and Period Style Analysis*, Frankfurt: Peter Lang, 2001.

23 On Odoevsky's career and activities, see Cornwell, 1986. On music in particular (Odoevsky as important critic, musicologist, music promoter, and even, in a small way, composer), see the chapter 'The Musician', ibid., pp. 121–59; see also Campbell, 1989.

24 For an examination of *Russian Nights*, see Cornwell, 1998, pp. 69–99. On Odoevsky's Romanticism, see ibid., pp. 33–68. See also Sucur, *Poe, Odoyevsky, and Purloined Letters*, who sees Odoevsky as closer to the late-Romantic, or Biedermeier, period style. On philosophy and Odoevsky in general, see Cornwell, 1986 ('The Thinker', pp. 74–120).

25 For 'Sebastian's inner life', the narrator claims: 'There is only one means to learn about these events. I advise you to play all Bach's music from beginning to end, as I did' (*RN*, 179 / 123). This may be compared with the comment of a twentieth-century biographer: 'Though few musicians' lives are outwardly more clearly accounted for than Bach's, as far as the documents go, we have never got to know a great deal about his inner life': W.R. Anderson, 'Johann Sebastian Bach', in A.L. Bacharach, ed., *The Lives of the Great Composers*, London: Gollancz, 1935, p. 17.

26 J.S. Bach's eldest brother, Johann Christoph Bach (1671–1721), who indeed held the family reins after the death of their parents, in fact lived until Sebastian was thirty-six. Odoevsky may have conflated him with another Johann Christoph Bach (1642–1703), a cousin of J.S. Bach's father.

27 Livingstone's translation is preferred here: *Art and Creativity*, 186; *SS*, 4, 406.

28 Elizabeth M. Butler, *The Fortunes of Faust* [1952], Stroud: Sutton Publishing, 1998: 'The First Faust Reborn, 1947', pp. 321–38 (p. 323).
29 This story by Odoevsky was translated several times into German, and into French, in the nineteenth century; *Sebastian Bach* was translated into German in 1924; *Russian Nights* as a full entity achieved its German translation only in 1970 (see Cornwell, 1986, p. 384).
30 Noted by Hannelore G. Mundt, '*Doktor Faustus*', The Literary Encyclopedia (posted 11 Sept. 2003). See www.litencyc.com/php/sworks.php?rec=true&UID=11472

References and further reading

Primary sources

Diderot, Denis, [1966] 1981, *Rameau's Nephew* and *D'Alembert's Dream*, trans. Leonard Tancock, Harmondsworth: Penguin.
Hoffmann, E.T.A., 'Ritter Gluck' and 'Councillor Krespel', in *Selected Writings of E.T.A. Hoffmann*, trans. Leonard J. Kent and Elizabeth C. Wright, Vol. 1, *The Tales*, pp. 49–59, 168–88 (also trans. as 'Rath Krespel'; and as 'The Cremona Violin'); *The Life and Opinions of Kater Murr*: Vol. 2, *The Novel*, Chicago and London: University of Chicago Press, 1969 (also trans. Anthea Bell as *The Life and Opinions of Tomcat Murr*, Harmondsworth: Penguin, 1999: *KM* in text).
Hoffmann, E.T.A., 1985, 'Don Giovanni' ('Don Juan'), in Heinrich von Kleist, Ludwig Tieck, E.T.A. Hoffmann, *Six German Romantic Tales*, trans. Ronald Taylor, London: Angel Books, pp. 104–17.
Hoffmann, E.T.A., 1989, *E.T.A. Hoffmann's Musical Writings: Kreisleriana, The Poet and the Composer, Music Criticism*, ed. David Charlton, trans. Martyn Clarke, Cambridge: Cambridge University Press (*HMW* in text).
Kleist, Heinrich von, 1978, 'St Cecilia or the Power of Music', in Kleist, *The Marquise of O- and Other Stories*, trans. David Luke and Nigel Reeves, Harmondsworth: Penguin, pp. 217–30.
Odoevskii, V.F., 1956, *Muzykal'no-literaturnoe nasledie*, ed. G. Bernandt, Moscow: Gos. muzykal'noe izdatel'stvo.
Odoevskii, V.F., 1975, *Russkie nochi*, Leningrad: Nauka,

'Literaturnye pamiatniki'; and 1981, *Sochineniia v dvukh tomakh*, Moscow: Khodozhestvennaia literatura vol. 1.

Odoevsky, Vladimir Fedorovich, 1965, *Russian Nights*, trans. Olga Koshansky-Olienikov and Ralph E. Matlaw, New York: Dutton; repr. with an afterword by Neil Cornwell, Evanston, IL: Northwestern University Press, 1997 (*RN* in text).

Pasternak, Alexander, 1984, *A Vanished Present: The Memoirs of Alexander Pasternak*, trans. Ann Pasternak Slater, Oxford: Oxford University Press.

Pasternak, Boris, 1986, *Suboctave Story* and *A Safe Conduct*, trans. Christopher Barnes, in Boris Pasternak, *The Voice of Prose, Volume One*, ed. Christopher Barnes, Edinburgh: Polygon, pp. 129–56; 21–108 (*VP* in text).

Pasternak, Boris, 1989–92, *Sobranie sochinenii v piati tomakh*, Moscow: Khudozhestvennaia literatura, 1989–92, ed. A.A. Voznesenskii et al. (*SS* in text).

Pasternak, Boris, 1990, 'People and Propositions', trans. Nicolas Pasternak-Slater; 'Seryozha's Story' and 'Chopin', trans. Christopher Barnes, in Boris Pasternak, *People and Propositions. The Voice of Prose: Volume Two*, ed. Christopher Barnes, Edinburgh: Polygon, pp. 26–87, 111–68, 274–8 (*PP* in text).

Wackenroder, W.H., 1971, *Confessions and Fantasies*, trans. M.H. Schubert, University Park: Pennsylvania State University Press.

Secondary sources

Barnes, Christopher, 1977, 'Boris Pasternak, the Musician-Poet and Composer', *Slavica Hierosolymitana*, 1, pp. 317–35.

Barnes, Christopher, 1989, *Boris Pasternak: A Literary Biography: Volume I, 1890–1928*, Cambridge: Cambridge University Press.

Campbell, James Stuart, 1989, *V.F. Odoyevsky and the Formation of Russian Musical Taste in the Nineteenth Century*, New York and London: Garland.

Cardinal, Roger, 1975, *German Romantics in Context*, London: Studio Vista.

Cornwell, Neil, 1986, *The Life, Times and Milieu of V.F. Odoyevsky, 1804–1869*, with a foreword by Sir Isaiah Berlin, London: Athlone Press and Athens, OH: Ohio University Press.

Cornwell, Neil, 1998, *Vladimir Odoevsky and Romantic Poetics: Collected Essays*, Providence and Oxford: Berghahn Books.

Di Simplicio, Daša Šilkánková, 1990, *La nascita di un poeta: Boris Pasternak*, Naples: Liguori Editore.

Evans-Romaine, Karen, 1997, *Boris Pasternak and the Tradition of German Romanticism*, Munich: Otto Sagner.

Fleishman, Lazar', 1981, *Boris Pasternak v dvadtsatye gody*, Munich: Wilhem Fink.

Greber, Erika, 1989, *Intertextualität und Interpretierbarkeit des Texts: Zu frühen Prosa Boris Pasternaks*, Munich: Wilhelm Fink.

Ljunggren, Anna, 1984, *Juvenilia Borisa Pasternaka: 6 fragmentov o Relinkvimini*, Stockholm: Almqvist and Wiksell.

Pasternak, E.B., 1977, 'Vstupitel'naia stat'ia' to Boris Pasternak, 'Istoriia odnoi kontroktavy', *Slavica Hierosolymitana*, 1, pp. 251–92 (pp. 251–6).

Rudova, Larissa, 1994, *Pasternak's Short Fiction and the Cultural Vanguard*, New York: Peter Lang.

Rudova, Larissa, 1997, *Understanding Boris Pasternak*, Columbia, SC: University of South Carolina Press.

2

Starman: the rise of the 'cosmic traveller'

Much science fiction is pure Romance. Romance is the story of an *elsewhere*.

(Umberto Eco, *Reflections on The Name of the Rose*)

Among examples in the relatively unusual genre of early works of Russian science fiction are to be found stories by Vladimir Odoevsky.[1] Two works of his are concerned with the impending catastrophic approach of a comet to the Earth. In an early story of just five pages, 'Two Days in the Life of the Terrestrial Globe' (*Dva dni v zhizni zemnogo shara*), written in 1825, Odoevsky starts off in society-tale mode, assumes an air of science fiction, and concludes with a Schellingian aura of benign apocalypse, in a merger of the earthly and the heavenly, the Earth and the Sun.[2] A first translation of this work is appended to this study. Much lengthier, though never completed, was *The Year 4338* (*4338-i god*) – a Utopian work set in the distant future when, again, a comet's impact is expected.[3] A minor link between Odoevsky and early western futuristic or science fiction is the review he published in 1827 of Mary Shelley's novel, *The Last Man* (1826). Odoevsky may also have known such pre- decessors as *L'an deux mille quatre cent quarante, rêve s'il en fut jamais* by Louis Sébastien Mercier (1771; expanded version, 1786) and Jean Cousin de Grainville's *Le dernier homme* (1805). Fragments of *The Year 4338* were published by Odoevsky in 1835 and 1840, but in its fullest surviving version the work first appeared only in 1926.[4]

The Year 4338 has been held to be remarkable enough, for its prediction of time travel (through an advanced form of Mesmerism) and for its now familiar technological advances (air and space travel, the telephone, photocopying – even the internet).[5] Odoevsky's *magnum opus*, the philosophical frame-tale novel *Russian Nights* (*Russkie nochi*, published in full in 1844), included two dystopian tales, or parables, 'The Last Suicide' and 'A City Without Name' (polemicising with the ideas of Malthus and Bentham respectively).[6] These comprise, or include, early examples of the concise potted history of a planet, or a civilisation, which was to become a familiar leitmotif in works such as Dostoevsky's *The Dream of a Ridiculous Man* (*Son smeshnogo cheloveka*) and, as we shall see, in subsequent science fiction. There is, however, another Odoevsky story – and not one bearing any overt stamp of science fiction – which, ironic as it may seem, may have had a more significant, if largely indirect, effect on the development of this form.

The Live Corpse (*Zhivoi mertvets*), dated 1838 but not published until 1844, was written towards the end of Odoevsky's main period of creative literary activity (which extended from the end of the 1820s until the early 1840s). The plot, such as it is, is unusual but simple. A middle-aged and successful civil servant, Vasilii Kuz'mich Aristidov, awakes one morning to find that he has died: 'What's this? – it seems I've died? . . . really!' (66 / 306).[7] This is the very beginning of the story, which continues in a colloquial, humorous style of first-person narrative, breaking from time to time into a form of dramatic dialogue somewhat reminiscent of Gogolian comedy: 'It's strange, very strange – the soul's splitting from the body!' (ibid.). The 'spirit' departs from the body, together with the soul, and observes the body lying on the bed 'as if nothing had happened' (ibid.). Looking in the mirror, it finds its mirror image has also departed (taking up a Hoffmannian motif). Gradually acclimatising to its new-found state, the 'spirit' is able to move around and observe other people, without being seen or heard by them.

Having been a man of regular habits, the 'spirit' steps out to the office as usual, and on the way is run down (or rather run through), with no ill effects, by a speeding carriage. The 'spirit', becoming aware of a facility to transport itself by flight to wherever it wants to go, is at first cheerful in its new freedom. Gradually, however, it becomes more and more depressed – from loneliness and alienation, and from the remarks and actions of its erstwhile colleagues, friends and family, which, despite attempted interjections, it is unable to influence. A series of picaresque wanderings and scenes involving those close to him in career and private life reveal, first to the reader and then to the 'spirit' of Aristidov himself, the falsity and shallowness of his self-satisfied complacency and open to view the sordid reality of a self-centred, materialistic life. More and more despairing as this self-awareness comes on, the 'spirit' finds that everyone is talking about him and exposing some aspect of his past life, or the consequences of his actions. Trying to escape this, he resorts to taking refuge in his grave and to flying around the world. Time and space are distorted, and events are nightmarishly telescoped. Finally, after Aristidov's son poisons his brother, and his niece Liza, who has been swindled out of her fortune by the brothers acting under the inspiration of Aristidov's example, has landed in jail and gone mad, Aristidov is assailed in an apocalyptic finale by the spirits of all those he has wronged. Presumably the abyss is to follow.

At this point, however, Aristidov wakes up, exclaiming: 'What a stupid dream!' (88 / 331). He berates the authors of tales such as the one he was reading the night before, and ends by wondering which of his mistresses he should go and see. The dream has obviously had no effect on him whatsoever.

Basically a 'society tale' with Gothic-Romantic trappings (the fantastic element of a 'ghost' telling the story), *The Live Corpse* is, like many of Odoevsky's stories, an amalgam of styles and devices, written with a number of intentions, to be read at a number of levels. It may first be read as a story of the fantastic, invoking reader hesitation as to the narrative's provenance, if the title is not an immediate give-away, until the dream explanation is revealed at the end. This abrupt revelation may indicate an element of pastiche, and a suspicion that Odoevsky is exploiting the genre by presenting his overall didactic and philosophical intentions within a fantastic framework. Social and moral satire is enclosed within both Hoffmannian and Sentimentalist parody,[8] with Gogolian touches and anticipations of the prose of the rising 'natural school' in Russia. At the same time, *The Live Corpse* serves as a vehicle for Odoevsky's attacks against the worship of reason (seen as early blasts in the Dostoevsky-Chernyshevsky debate that was to rage in the 1860s) and for the promotion of his ethical and philosophical concerns.[9] Aristidov's dream is a vision of immortality, or at least of an indeterminate period following death, as a journey through one's own conscience, during which the consequences (actual or possible) of a whole life and all its component actions unfold. Such a state of spiritual 'survival' after death, in an unusually modern presentation, provokes comparison with the existential tendencies of later writers, from Dostoevsky onward into the next century.

Not only did Dostoevsky know Odoevsky personally (and may have used him as a prototype for Prince X in his *Netochka Nezvanova*, as noted in the previous chapter), but he clearly knew *The Live Corpse*, as he in fact used the following lines from it as the epigraph to his first published work of fiction, *Poor Folk* (or *Poor People: Bednye liudi*, 1846):

> Oh, these story tellers! They can't write something useful, pleasant, soothing! They have to dig up all the dirty tricks under the sun! They ought to be forbidden to write! Well, I mean to say! You read it and let it sink in – and then all kinds of balderdash enter your head; really, they should be forbidden to write, simply forbidden altogether . . . (88 / 330–1)

Certain of Dostoevsky's pre-exile works contain fantastic-Romantic elements (*The Double*, *The Landlady*, and *Netochka Nezvanova*) and a number of commentators have pointed to an influence here from Odoevsky, as well as from Hoffmann. There is, however, generally held to be a comparative lack of these elements in Dostoevsky's later work, until they re-emerge in somewhat different form in the trio of fantastic stories written in the 1870s: *Bobok* (1873), *A Gentle Creature* (*Krotkaia*, 1876) and *The Dream of a Ridiculous Man* (1877). Of these three stories, only *Bobok* and *The Dream of a Ridiculous Man* approach the fantastic in the Todorovian sense of reader hesitation, and even these arguably remain rooted in 'reality', in so far as *Bobok* is explained from the outset as attributable to demented alcoholic ravings, while the title does at least seem to indicate the provenance of the third and last story.

More appropriate to these stories, including *The Live Corpse*, may be the model of Menippean satire (as expounded by Bakhtin and by Northrop Frye). In addition to a philosophical intent, present in *The Live Corpse* and particularly so in *The Dream of a Ridiculous Man*, Menippean satire and fantastic literature share such qualities as the prominence of dream, an artistic conception of space and time, and an element of self-parody. In Dostoevsky's story, resemblances with *The Live Corpse* – even if not at first sight all that obvious – are in fact both widespread and complex, operating on three levels: similarity, inversion and development (ideas or motifs found in Odoevsky, which are developed or enlarged by Dostoevsky).

The most striking similarity is, of course, the use of dream in the structure of each story to highlight consciousness and to facilitate psychological penetration (in both cases, with results verging on the psychoanalytic). In Odoevsky, Aristidov continually questions whether he is really dead; in Dostoevsky, there is great stress on the Ridiculous Man's awareness of being dead. In both cases, following 'death', the 'spirits' are able to observe what is happening in the life they have left behind, their own burial and so on. Aristidov's observation of this is from an objective standpoint external to the body; the Ridiculous Man's is subjective. Similar too are Odoevsky's (perhaps slightly lesser) stress on the role of falsity in the downfall of human life, and Dostoevsky's insistence on the primacy of lying in all human and social failings. The motifs of flight and distortion of space-time also figure in both, the scale of these being immensely enlarged by Dostoevsky. Everyone is talking about Aristidov (in death), while everyone laughed at the Ridiculous Man (in life, both before and after the dream); this is accompanied by a feeling of alienation and loneliness (Aristidov in death, the Ridiculous Man in life).

Two main inversions can be picked out. Aristidov develops a feeling of guilt and conscience only after death, and this has vanished on his return to life, after the dream. The Ridiculous Man, on the other hand, starts to feel responsibility and guilt before his death, at the time of committing suicide; these feelings play an important part in his dream, and they are felt even more deeply after the dream. Based on this, we can say that Aristidov's dream has no lasting effect on him, and this may therefore suggest a pessimistic element in the author's philosophy. The Ridiculous Man, in contrast, is transformed by the intensity of his vision, by its essential 'truth', and is led to a position of (albeit irrational) optimism.

Dostoevsky's enlargement of the scope and scale of flight, and of temporal-spatial disorder, has already been mentioned. Similar treatment by Dostoevsky of themes or ideas found in Odoevsky can also be instanced. The Utopian aspect of *The Dream of a Ridiculous Man* may well owe something in origin to Odoevsky's futuristic and anti-Utopian tales. Odoevsky's attack on the cult of rationality has also been mentioned above, while Dostoevsky's comments on 'a modern Russian progressive' (729 / 113) and the final stress on the 'living image' (737 / 118) of what the Ridiculous

Man has seen (as opposed to an abstract concept arrived at by reason) are a demonstration of his well-known stand on this issue.[10] Allied to this, and again carried further by Dostoevsky, is Odoevsky's idea of the loss of instinctual energy caused by the development of reason and culture. The natural lifestyle (before their Fall) of the people visited by the Ridiculous Man was just what mankind, according to Odoevsky, had lost and should strive to reattain, though not by totally obviating science and reason. What was required was a new synthesis, a fusion of knowledge and culture with an all-embracing new and poetic type of science, in which the aesthetic would play its part, and nature in its full sense would be grasped.

Aristidov's gradual realisation of guilt, at least within his dream, is developed in the case of the Ridiculous Man. The latter indeed takes on responsibility for the wholesale corruption of the entire paradise he is visiting, the complete wrecking of a Golden Age, and, in a somewhat grotesque role as an Antichrist, he demands to be crucified. This demand is greeted with contempt and he is branded a madman. Nevertheless, the concentration on the examination of a single life in *The Live Corpse* is expanded to seemingly gigantic proportions in *The Dream of a Ridiculous Man*, not just to cover the life of the protagonist himself, but to comprise an allegory of world history.

The hints of existential speculation in Odoevsky take on a greater prominence in Dostoevsky's story. Before the dream takes place, the Ridiculous Man explains his feeling of its making 'no difference' ('*vsyo ravno*') 'whether the world existed or whether nothing existed anywhere at all' (718 / 105). This idea he carries to the point of ultimate nihilism, denying all existence – past, present and future:

> I began to be acutely conscious that *nothing existed in my own lifetime*. At first I couldn't help feeling that at any rate in the past many things had existed; but later on I came to the conclusion that there had not been anything even in the

past, but that for some reason it had merely seemed to have been. Little by little I became convinced that there would be nothing in the future, either. (ibid.)

As the moment of intended suicide approaches, inspired by a 'little star' (719–20 / 106) he speculates that, when the world ends for him, maybe the world will end altogether. Then, approaching the point of relating his dream, he says:

> What does it matter whether it was a dream or not, so long as that dream revealed the Truth to me? For once you have recognised the truth and seen it, you know that it is the one and only truth and that there can be no other, whether you are dreaming it or living it. (724 / 109; translation adapted)

The question of the nature of dream as a transcendental mystical experience, in which 'death' is a way to a new 'life' and back again to 'reality', suggesting the possibility of parallel lives, probabilities and visions of alternative realities, albeit schematised or allegorical, is present first in Odoevsky and is developed almost forty years later by Dostoevsky. This he may be said to be doing in a surprisingly modern (or modernist) manner, posing some of the same questions on the nature of reality, the illusory *maya* of this life and a transcendental alternative, that were to be raised in the twentieth century by writers such as Herman Hesse (in *Steppenwolf* and 'The Indian Life' from *The Glass Bead Game*). The motifs of supposed death, or pre-suicide exposition, are to be taken up again in Sigizmund Krzhizhanovsky's remarkable story *Autobiography of a Corpse* (1925); the decline of civilisation is also treated, this time in a satirical manner, in the same author's *Yellow Coal*.[11]

Dostoevsky himself returns briefly to space travel soon after *The Dream of a Ridiculous Man*, in his last novel *The Karamazov Brothers* (1879–80). Ivan Karamazov's visiting 'shabby devil' (or *alter ego*) 'had to travel through all of outer space before [he] could reach earth . . . of course, it only takes a moment'; this entity also adds that 'the earth itself may have been recycled a billion times over . . . It's a dreadful bore'.[12] It is not coincidental that similar elements enter Mann's *Doctor Faustus* (see *DF*, 261–2). Somewhat similarly, Chekhov's eponymous black monk (of 1894) wanders through space and time with no boundaries: 'Having left the earth's atmosphere behind at last, he now wanders through the entire universe, never encountering conditions which would enable him to fade away. Perhaps he's to be seen on Mars somewhere, now, or on some star of the Southern Cross' (Chekhov, 1989, 75).

These three works (especially the first) will feature again in rather more detail in Chapter 4 of this study. Much more recently, Orhan Pamuk (a keen reader of Dostoevsky and Chekhov, among many other European writers) has victims describing their own murders, one such corpse commenting on his own funeral, and posthumous 'crossings' of the soul taking 'thousands of years, though it seemed no more than the blink of an eye' (*My Name is Red*, 1998, p. 277).

*   *   *   *

As in earlier versions of what now forms the first part of the present chapter, I am extending the discussion of these two stories by Odoevsky and Dostoevsky to forge a comparison with the poetic treatments of flying and the persistent use of a dream-reality dichotomy in Maiakovsky's narrative poems *Man* (*Chelovek*) and *About That* (*Pro eto*).[13] Spatio-temporal distortions, utilised by Odoevsky and expanded to cosmic proportions by Dostoevsky, are taken up in a similar vein by Maiakovsky. Russian Futurist poetry will therefore provide us with a kind of modernist poetic intermission, before we embark upon a change of direction, to introduce English science fiction and further cosmic dreamers (or purported travellers).

Strong links between Dostoevsky's works and Maia-kovsky's *About That* (the reference to Raskolnikov, line 1137, is immediately striking) are well known.[14] In particu-lar, links are pinpointed between the last section of the

Maiakovsky poem ('A request in the name of . . .') and *The Dream of a Ridiculous Man*.[15] What this section seeks to suggest, then, is that certain motifs and ideas to be located in the stories by Odoevsky and Dostoevsky undergo further expansion and development in fantastic poetical form in Maiakovsky's *Man* and *About That*.

About That (1923) stands somewhat apart from much of Maiakovsky's poetry of the Soviet period, and can be seen in many ways as a second part, a thematic continuation and a reappraisal of *Man* (written some seven years earlier, in 1916–17). The latter narrative poem is arguably the most important and the most complex of Maiakovsky's pre-Revolutionary works. For present purposes, the two can be considered together.

In comparing these poems with the prose stories in question, the first problem to arise is the nature of the fantastic in relation to poetry. Poetry, in Tzvetan Todorov's view, is a genre in which normal representation is in any case rejected, and therefore the fantastic, in the sense in which we might understand it here, cannot arise.[16] This lack of the possibility of the fantastic in one sense leaves the poet completely free. 'Fantastic-type' elements may be introduced without any concern, unlike in prose, for questions of artificiality in the placing of the boundaries between the 'fantastic' and the 'realistic'.

Maiakovsky exploits this freedom to the full in his poetry, by the introduction of fantastic elements, vast expansions and contractions of scale, hyperbole and surrealistic imagery. He is therefore able to insert a fantastic motif such as flight without of necessity having recourse to a framework of dream, death or illusion. When the suicide theme comes to the fore in *Man*, the hero (the poet himself) looks for a chemist to obtain poison, but then immediately claims that as man, 'your fantastic guest',[17] is immortal, poison is not necessary. In other words, death is not a prerequisite for the introduction of such a fantastic event as the passing from one 'life' to another.

> A dim realisation came over the fool.
> Gapers seen through windows.
> My hair stands on end.
> And suddenly I
> Sail lightly past the counter.
> The ceiling opens up by itself. (I, pp. 257–8, ll. 436–41)

There then proceeds a fantastic ascent to heaven without death having to occur first, even nominally.

There are a number of features common to *The Dream of a Ridiculous Man* and the Maiakovsky poems, which are not shared by *The Live Corpse*. The most obvious of these is the suicide theme. Others include the presence of Christ figures, the motif of the star (present in *Man* in the 'The Birth of Maiakovsky' section, and at the very end of the poem), and the 'Ruler of All' (*Povelitel' vsego*), whose origin may owe something to Dostoevsky's similarly named figure (*vlastitel' vsego*), to whom the Ridiculous Man makes an appeal (110 / 726).

Apart from the obvious motif of 'flying' and the persistent use of dream-reality (particularly in *About That* it is often difficult to pinpoint exactly when one dream sequence ends and what passes for reality begins), there are a number of elements common to the works under consideration. Spatio-temporal distortions, present in Odoevsky, and expanded to cosmic proportions by Dostoevsky, are continued in the same vein by Maiakovsky, with, in addition, vast projections forward in time. On a more minor level, the paranoia arising from the feeling of everyone talking about Aristidov, carried on through the Ridiculous Man, crops up again in *About That*, when Maiakovsky, eavesdropping at a party, thinks everyone is talking about him (IV, p. 168, ll. 1179–92).

The comparatively veiled attack on reason in Odoevsky, somewhat more explicit in Dostoevsky, is replaced in *About That* by the attack on *byt*. This is a Russian word of complex connotations, including, in the Maiakovsky context of the 1920s, the tedious detail of everyday life; detested or ridiculed aspects of bourgeois lifestyle (symbolised in *About That* by tea-drinking); everything Maiakovsky had been railing at in his pre-Revolutionary poetry, from *A Cloud in Trousers* (*Oblako in shtanakh*) and before, to *Man*; plus, and in particular, the survival and re-emergence of all these elements in the new Soviet state (bureaucracy, petty-mindedness, philistinism, etc., as exemplified in the spirit of the New Economic Policy). Maiakovsky's attack on the all-pervasive concept of *byt*, the creeping philistinism rising again from within, and the final recognition of its presence in himself, bear a close resemblance to, and may be seen as an expansion of, Odoevsky's attack on the demon of materialism and the worship of money in *The Live Corpse*. Nevertheless, the class orientation of these two writers leads to an essential difference of emphasis: Maiakovsky's demon attacks humanity as a whole, especially the poor and working classes, whereas Odoevsky's strikes at the comparatively rich and powerful. The significance to Maiakovsky of the phenomenon of *byt*, together with his at least partial disillusionment with aspects of the situation at this time, was a vital factor. *About That* is also Maiakovsky's defence of himself as a poet under siege from the new philistinism, in the person of the proletarian poets, which was to destroy him in the poem, as, eventually, it would in life. This takes on an almost metaphysical force when combined with his preoccupations with the human condition in the form of what one critic has called 'cosmic alienation', leading in *Man* and *About That* to a state of existential and metaphysical rebellion.[18] Thus the existential musings present in embryo in Odoevsky and developed by Dostoevsky find their fullest expression here in Maiakovsky, in his search for 'the man on the bridge', the Maiakovsky of 1916, who, suicide-prone then as later, had been left suspended in cosmic revolt, refusing to accept either the idea of progress in this world or a bodiless existence in the next.

Maiakovsky is not hostile to reason as such, as are, in varying degrees, Odoevsky and Dostoevsky, but he does have extreme difficulty sustaining any faith in progress, sinking into ultimate despair in *Man*, rising again to a new-found scientific and Utopian optimism at the end of *About That*, only for this to pale somewhat in his play *The Bedbug* (*Klop*, 1928), and, tragically, to disappear altogether by the end of the decade. The 'rational optimism' of *About That* is perhaps best seen as a kind of 'ultimate Futurism', by which all hopes – namely the triad of faith, hope and love – are placed in a new Golden Age of the thirtieth century. Then man not only will be able to, but *will* by scientific means effect, at least in selected cases, a physical resurrection of the dead. This startling idea probably derives from the views of the Russian philosopher N.F. Fedorov (1828–1903), and it may be noted that Fedorov's stress on the application of science to moral problems, indeed a new approach to the idea of science (harnessing it to the 'common cause'), is not far removed from, and may well owe something to, Odoevsky's ideas on science.[19] In any case, there is certainly common ground between the overall synthesis sought in Odoevsky's ultimate philosophical aims, Dostoevsky's final goal of love and universal brotherhood, and Maiakovsky's Utopian optimism at the end of *About That*. At this point, love will abandon its former sordid state and, ranging far beyond personification in Maiakovsky's beloved Lilia, will cover the universe in brotherhood and harmony (IV, pp. 183–4, ll. 1761–813).

*   *   *   *   *

In 1908 William Hope Hodgson published *The House on the Borderland*. This novel, according to Mike Ashley, was 'inspired by H.G. Wells's *The Time Machine* (1895)' and 'involves a house on a transdimensional threshold' whose occupant ('the old Recluse': Hodgson, 1988, 9) is 'haunted by strange hog-like creatures and then drawn into a vision of the far future' (Ashley, 1997, 471). Brian Aldiss (1986,

167) sees this work, together with Hodgson's epic fantasy *The Night Land* (1912), as 'scientific romances' containing highly impressive embedded visions. Aldiss (168) rates this particular 'mystical vision', 'a mingling of astronomy and psychic experience', as 'a bravura piece of writing, full of wonder, . . . bursting far beyond the tawdry horror story in which it is set'.[20] We shall return again to the word 'vision'. Another commentator, Amanda Boulter, notes the narrative action as alternating between 'earth battles and hallucinogenic adventures in space' enabling 'a cosmic, pseudo-scientific journey to Heaven and Hell' (Boulter, 1993, 27; see also the 'Introduction to the Manuscript' by the 'Editor', as which Hodgson poses: Hodgson, 1988, 9–10).

This doubly framed 'MS' (which is reduced at a central point, by dint of 'illegibility', to 'Fragments': 83–4), if taken in isolation, is temporally and geographically 'unplaceable' (according to Boulter, 1993, 28). The fact of its being discovered in a remote part of the west of Ireland (by two apparently English, or more probably Welsh, visitors), before being passed much later to the author-editor, chimes with the Irish settings to a number of Hodgson's other works (notwithstanding his Essex origins).[21] It also, however, suggests an underlying subtheme of Irish colonialism (remarked on by Boulter, 1993, 28–9). The eponymous 'borderland', however, has nothing – at least, of itself here – to do with pre-partition Ireland, but represents rather the textual and sexual, as well as the dimensional, cultural and epochal borderlands that can invite, too, a psychoanalytical reading (see ibid., 32–3). The Recluse himself refers to the mystery of having 'penetrated within the borderland of some unthought of region – some subtle, intangible place, or form, of existence' (Hodgson, 1988, 112). The words 'abyss' and 'chasm' frequently occur, and the 'House' (the Recluse is particular, if not necessarily consistent, in his use of capitals) stands out on approach as 'that awesome Pile' (120). The (in reality authorial) Editor, in reading the MS, had 'lifted the Curtains of the Impossible', having from the outset derived 'an impression of the fantastic' (9).

We are here, though, more concerned with the phenomenon of cosmic, or be it 'astral' travel – which may, or may not, have anything to do with the 'astral body' as propounded by Paracelsus.[22] The same house apparently figures, or doubles, at one end of the universe and at the other – as do certain other 'natural' features, a 'Pit' and a 'Plain', with which it is said to be '*en rapport* – to use a recognised term' (121). 'Travel' (if such it be) is somehow effected into and through outer space, and/or from one dimension to another, or across parallel universes. 'Somehow' is here the operative word, as any exact nature of this motion remains unclear throughout, as Hodgson's Recluse (unlike the narrators in the stories by Odoevsky and Dostoevsky) – and seemingly deliberately – avoids use of the verb 'to fly'. From the one house and plain to the other, at first 'hovering' and 'looking down', then 'outside', 'floating', as 'a fragile flake of souldust', he 'moved' (25). 'Onwards, outwards, I drove', the earth receding behind, and 'flickered silently across the void', passing 'beyond the fixed stars' and 'still I fled onward', before finally 'descending' and landing (25–6). Even there, he was 'being borne forward' to 'the place, towards which I was being conveyed' (26). Back too the Recluse 'was borne', 'mounted higher', 'had risen' and eventually 'neared the earth's surface' (31–2). Subsequent journeyings are similarly marked: 'I journeyed back', 'I sped across', 'flitting swiftly' (83–4). Earlier it seemed to be a corporeal form of transport; later, however, 'I was a bodyless thing' (95), subjected to 'soul-wandering' (113).

What the Recluse describes as 'that strange and terrible journey through space and time' (referring here only to one of such forays: 123) thus represents huge temporal-spatial distortions – even by comparison to what appears to occur in the earlier stories discussed above. Journeys 'back once more to the known universe' (83), or 'among the Outer Worlds', which appear to take aeons of time, can be accomplished within a modest absence from the 'home' dimension of 'nearly a day and a night' (34). The Recluse's '*account* or *story*, whichever it may be' (italics in the original; and Hodgson confesses to 'an inclination to use the first term': 9) can be said, in any event, it might be added, to recount what 'happens' to the Recluse, rather than what he 'does'. One chapter is entitled, and duly then describes, 'The End of the Solar System' (108–11). The cosmic travel, dream or spiritual journey (whatever it may be), past 'dead stars' and a 'Green Sun', which seems to have black hole qualities, enables him to enter an 'impalpable globule', passing 'into some further, and, until then, invisible dimension' (111, 116).

On his first peregrination, the Recluse is suddenly conscious that 'a single star broke its way through the darkness' (32). Later he recalls being 'unaccountably attracted' to a 'luminous globe', while a 'White Orb' seen 'hidden in the shadow of the Sun of Darkness' might or might not be 'one and the same' as the 'Green Sun' (116). Such stellar sightings may by now seem reminiscent of the Ridiculous Man's 'little star', which had 'inspired' that figure to determine upon suicide. The Recluse's entire saga seems to be epitomised in the statement: 'Visions of the Unnamable rose, vaguely' (117). Furthermore, the Recluse's attitude to his 'vision' – 'the vision – if vision it were' (25); 'that vision (though, even now, I doubt whether it was a vision)' (47) – will also remind readers of the Ridiculous Man's questioning of the status of his dream: 'What does it matter whether it was a dream or not . . .?'. In Hodgson, the Recluse, were it not for certain factors (such as the life and death mini-saga of his dog Pepper – though, curiously, his sister appears little affected), 'should . . . be inclined to imagine that it was but a gigantic dream' (123). It should also be mentioned that 1877, the year of the discovery of the MS (see the novel's subtitle), as well as being the year of Hodgson's birth, happens to be the year that *The Dream of a Ridiculous Man* was originally published.[23]

*   *   *   *   *

Olaf Stapledon's narrator follows Hodgson's Recluse into space, in somewhat similar style, at the beginning of the novel *Star Maker* (1937; Stapledon, 1988; hereafter *SM*). This occurs, again, by means of what is ostensibly a dream. Indeed, we might note, 'dream' and 'travel' appear to be conjoined phenomena in many such works, as prodigious travel advances towards the supposed actual travel of modern science fiction. This seems to be the case once more here, as the purportedly authorial narrator starts from, and finishes back upon, the heather on a suburban hillside, within sight of his house one night, having 'tasted bitterness' at home and in the world and 'horror at our futility' (*SM*, 11). In a way that is similar to parallel key moments in Dostoevsky and Hodgson, 'obscurity unveiled a star' overhead (12), and, as the journey (or vision) gets under way, the narrator wonders if he 'had died and was entering some wholly unexpected new existence' (17). He returns at the striking of midnight on what would seem to be the same night (257). What has 'happened' in between is indeed extraordinary. Brian Aldiss (1986, 195) calls it 'a new – and so far unsurpassed – version of the spiritual voyage'; to Robert Crossley, *Star Maker* is a 'theological romance', containing 'dazzlingly baroque theological speculations' (Crossley, 1994, 114, 166).

The narrating protagonist (if such he may be called)[24] alights first on a parallel Earth-type planet, which he terms the Other Earth. There, in Dostoevskian fashion, he is witness to the rise and fall of civilisation, although, unlike the Ridiculous Man, this visiting narrator has no personal involvement in the course of these events. Leaving aside for the moment the modes of travel, the narrator achieves his understanding through the passive 'inhabiting' of native individuals, resulting in 'internal "telepathic" intercourse' (*SM*, 34). Such a process is then extended to 'telepathic exploration' much further afield in space and time through, or along with, at first one like-minded fellow traveller (together with Bvalltu of the Other Earth, comprising 'two disembodied minds': 70) and eventually many of them.

As with *The House on the Borderland*, the mode of travel is kept unspecified, at least at first, with an initial avoidance of use of the verb 'to fly' or of any clear system of propulsion. The narrator here can be 'soaring away' (17), or just 'travelling' (18), 'still travelling' as 'speed increased' (22); though soon enough this has become 'my new power of locomotion' (25). Direction, or destination, can be determined 'by merely willing to approach a star' (25); out among the stars 'I was a disembodied, wandering viewpoint' (29); as such, 'I glided with wingless flight' (32). A bit later, however, this 'disembodied flight through space' is said to be practised through 'psychical attraction', by means of 'telepathic projection of the mind directly into some alien world' (71). The whole saga is seen as 'a voyage of astronomical and metaphysical research' (25), or even 'a high pilgrimage' (27), whose purpose 'was not merely scientific observation, but also the need to effect some kind of mental and spiritual traffic with other worlds, for mutual enrichment and community' (34). It is through a 'kind of internal "telepathic" intercourse' that wanderings here and further afield are to take place (34–5). Later, we hear of 'rocket-flight in space' (149), and elaborate interstellar travel through 'the treasure of sub-atomic energy' (150). In many ways, it reads like a more scientific version of Hodgson: Aldiss (1986, 195) notes the contributions therein of Einstein and modern astronomy.

In fact the concept of humans flying was a matter of serious interest to Stapledon. A very brief history of the Earth, given in a paragraph of *Star Maker*, 'lasting only for a few moments in the life of the galaxy' (*SM*, 185; see ch. 10, 'A Vision of the Galaxy': 178–87), alludes to his earlier solar-system saga, *Last and First Men* (1930). In this, Stapledon's first major novel, the Earth's population has to migrate first to Venus and then to Neptune, undergoing (or undertaking) a series of eighteen mutations of the human species. Of these, 'the seventh men' are a winged variety, engineered by their predecessor in the chain, equipped to develop a rich civilisation on 'the hot-island world' of the inner planet. Calling this work 'an essay in myth creation', Stapledon had built elaborately on the story of Icarus.[25]

Stapledon's elaborations and distortions of space and time expand far beyond anything seen in the previous works. At an early stage, the narrator's sense of time is soon utterly confused: 'Minutes and hours, and perhaps even days, even weeks, were now indistinguishable' (20). 'So rapidly did time pass before us', in the narrator's 'mature' collective travels, 'that aeons were packed into moments' (183). As 'utopia' develops, it is spread to form a 'great communal enterprise of worlds' (185) – 'The Galactic Society of Worlds' (188). The existence of highly successful races leads thus to 'minded worlds' (188), and furthermore to 'minded stars' (194) with purposeful activity, joining in a 'galactic dance' (198). In an expanding universe, 'the whole life of the cosmos', rather than basking in eternity, becomes conceived 'as a brief, headlong and forlorn, race against galloping time' (211). What has become 'the single, fully awakened spirit of the cosmos' (178) has taken on an expansion too of the Schellingian aura. From the end to the beginning: the narrator eventually has made contact 'not with micro-organisms, nor yet with worlds or stars with galactic minds, but with the minds of the great nebulae before their substance had disintegrated into stars to form the galaxies' (213).

He now regards himself, in some sense, as 'the incipient mind of the cosmos as a whole' (219). Watching 'all the lives of stars and worlds, and of the galactic communities', the narrator ultimately 'stood, confronted by the infinity that men call God' (226). This is – the eponymous and aloof Star Maker. The entire creation, destruction and re-creation of the cosmos, or the cosmic sequence, is in the gift, or at the whim, of the Star Maker. Thus: 'the virtue of the creator was to create, and to be infinite, the unrealizable and incomprehensible goal of worshipping creatures' (228). A force, or a being, 'incomparably greater than creativity', the Star Maker poses as 'the eternally achieved perfection of the absolute spirit' (224). There may here be some slight satisfaction, albeit at an infinitely distant level, for perhaps a minority of the avowedly more aberrant supporters of theories of 'intelligent design': there would certainly be none for 'creationists'.[26]

The Star Maker, in his 'maturity', went in for yet stranger forms of creation:

> These beings experienced their cosmos in a very odd manner. Living for a brief period along one dimension, each perceived at every moment of its life a simultaneous vista which, though of course fragmentary and obscure, was actually a view of a whole unique 'transverse' cosmical evolution in the other dimension. In some cases a creature had an active life in every temporal dimension of the cosmos. (251)

From the Icarus-type flight dream in Odoevsky's *The Live Corpse* (which Stapledon, one assumes, could not have known), to the inter-planetary motion and civilisation-fall of *The Dream of a Ridiculous Man* (which he certainly may well have known) and even the 'astral travel' of Hodgson (which surely he did know), to the cosmic voyaging of the narrator of *Star Maker*, is a highly impressive imaginative leap.

Stapledon, a part-time philosophy teacher, may hint at a debt to Dostoevsky (though here to *The Notes from Underground*) in his remark that the Star Maker 'could not, for instance, make twice two equal five' (234). Or perhaps he alludes to *The Dream of a Ridiculous Man*, and to Dostoevsky more generally, in his references to multiple Christ figures ('all the Christs of all the worlds': 137). Without here referring to Dostoevsky, Brian Aldiss – almost celebrating its neglect – calls *Star Maker* 'really the one great grey holy book of science fiction' (Aldiss, 1986, 199). Pamuk's *My*

Name is Red has already been mentioned in a somewhat similar, other-religious, context.

A more orthodox brand of science fiction descended, of course, by way of works by Edgar Allan Poe, Jules Verne and H.G. Wells (and one should certainly not forget the name of David Lindsay), intersecting again in Stapledon, passing down to the more serious and interesting of modern practitioners, such as Stanislaw Lem, the Strugatsky brothers, Arthur C. Clarke, Philip K. Dick and Ursula K. Le Guin. However, there are passages within Stapledon's work, such as the last one cited above, which, together with his successively sketched cosmological permutations, form not only a gamut of possibilities for science fictional worlds; on a more localised level, Stapledon's texts can read almost like programmatic statements for postmodernist fiction.

Notes

1 See Leland Fetzer's anthology (Fetzer, 1982) for a selection of this material, in English translation, from the nineteenth and early twentieth centuries.

2 Published in 1828, this story was reprinted in the collection *Vzgliad skvoz' stoletiia: russkaia fantastika XVIII i pervoi poloviny XIX veka*, ed. V. Guminsky, Moscow: Molodaia gvardiia, 1977, pp. 217–22.

3 It had been computed in the 1820s that the comet Biela would strike the Earth in the year 4339. The comet in question, in fact, burned up later in the nineteenth century.

4 A translation of this work appears in Fetzer (1982), and is reprinted in *Worlds Apart: An Anthology of Russian Fantasy and Science Fiction*, ed. Alexander Levitsky, New York, Woodstock, London: Overlook Duckworth, 2007. The original was also reprinted in Guminsky, pp. 240–74, and elsewhere (see below). It is discussed by Suvin (1979, 245–7) as an early European SF work of some importance.

5 See: 'Blogging predicted by 19th Century Russian Prince', www.mosnews.com. 10.10.2005.

6 On these stories, see ch. 6 of Cornwell, 1998, 120–35 (esp. pp. 127–33).

7 Page references are (respectively) to my English translation (in *The Salamander and Other Gothic Tales*; Odoevsky, 1992) and to *Povesti i rasskazy* (Odoevsky, 1959).

8 The play on 'Poor Liza' evokes the famous Sentimentalist tale of that name by Karamzin (*Bednaia Liza*, 1792).

9 These matters, in relation to this story, are discussed in much greater detail in ch. 2 of Cornwell, 1998, 11–29, from which the present material (on Odoevsky, pp. 11–18; and Dostoevsky, pp. 18–22) is excerpted or summarised. Elements from the thought of Fichte, Schopenhauer and Schelling are seen as contributing to Odoevsky's thought.

10 Page references are to the English translation and to vol. 25 of Dostoevsky's complete works respectively (see below).

11 Rediscovered stories by Sigizmund Krzhizhanovsky are collected in his *Seven Stories* (Krzhizhanovsky, 2006; for these works, see pp. 81–120, 184–202).

12 'The Devil. Ivan Fyodorovich's Nightmare', in Dostoevsky, *The Karamazov Brothers*, 1994, pp. 796–816 (pp. 802–3, 808).

13 See Cornwell, 1998, 21–5.

14 All references are to the Maiakovsky edition cited in the References below. This work (*About That* is the title most commonly accorded in English criticism) has been translated as 'About This' (by Herbert Marshall, in his edited *Mayakovsky and His Poetry*, 1942; new edition as *Mayakovsky*, London: Dobson, 1965); and as 'It' (by Dorian Rottenberg, in Mayakovsky, *Selected Works*, vol. 2, Moscow: Raduga, 1986). Rottenberg translates *Chelovek* as *Man*. For sources on the 'strong links', see Cornwell, 1998, 28–9, n. 42.

15 See Edward J. Brown, *Mayakovsky: A Poet in the Revolution*, Princeton: Princeton University Press, 1973, pp. 248–56.

16 In Todorov's words, if 'representation' as such be rejected, 'the fantastic *could not appear*: for the fantastic requires a reaction to events as they appear in the world evoked. For this reason, the fantastic can subsist only within fiction; poetry cannot be fantastic': Tzvetan Todorov, *The Fantastic: A Structural Approach to a Literary Genre*, trans. Richard Howard, Cleveland and London: The Press of Case Western Reserve University, 1973, p. 60.

17 The Russian word used (*nebyvalyi*) means 'unprecedented' or 'imaginary', as well as 'fantastic'. Conceivably, an apt translation here would be 'poetic'.

18 Lawrence Stahlberger, *The Symbolic System of Majakovskii*, The Hague: Mouton, 1964, p. 63.

19 Odoevsky's development as a thinker, including remarks concerning science, is summarised in Cornwell, 1986 (ch. 2, esp. pp. 75–90; and ch. 4, pp. 162–9). For a discussion of links between the thought of Fedorov, Dostoevsky and Maiakovsky, see Brown, *Mayakovsky*, pp. 253–5.

20 The 'horror' element, largely concerning apparent invasions by swine-like creatures, is somewhat reminiscent (or, rather, anticipatory) of 'The Hog', a story in Hodgson's *Carnacki the Ghost-Finder* (1913).

21 The novel has indeed a long subtitle: 'From the Manuscript discovered in 1877 by Messrs. Tonnison and Berreggnog, in the Ruins that lie to the South of the Village of Kraighten, in the West of Ireland. Set out here, with Notes' (Hodgson, 1988). Hodgson's authorial 'editorial' introduction is issued from Cardiganshire.

22 Paracelsus: i.e., Theophrast Bombast von Hohenheim (1493–1541). Swiss pysician and esoteric philosopher; his works were well known to a number of 'Romantic' writers, from Hoffmann, to Odoevsky, to Huysmans.

23 Although some readers – the present author included – may find it hard to conceive that Hodgson may not have known *The Dream of a Ridiculous Man*, any such connection would appear hard to prove. The first English translation of Dostoevsky's story that I have so far been able to uncover dates from 1916.

24 'Judged by the standards of the Novel,' Stapledon disarmingly asserts in the preface to his 'imaginative sketch', 'it [*Star Maker*] is remarkably bad. In fact, it is no novel at all' (*SM*, 8, 9).

25 Olaf Stapledon, *Last and First Men*, Harmondsworth: Penguin, 1987. See also 'The Flying Men from *Last and First Men*', excerpted in Crossley, *Stapledon Reader*, 1997, 3–11.

26 Indeed, Stapledon's conception of the 'supreme being', as Aldiss points out (1986, 197), 'was bound to upset Christians such as C.S. Lewis'. On the writing and reception of *Star Maker*,

see Crossley, 1994, 239–50. Similarly, see Stapledon's *Flames: A Fantasy*, in Crossley, 1997, 71–124 (esp. pp. 100, 121).

References and further reading

Primary sources

Chekhov, Anton, 1989, *A Woman's Kingdom and other Stories*, trans. Ronald Hingley, Oxford: Oxford University Press; *The Black Monk* (pp. 70–96).

Crossley, Robert, ed., *An Olaf Stapledon Reader*, 1997, Syracuse, NY: Syracuse University Press.

Dostoevsky, F.M., 1983, *Polnoe sobranie sochinenii v tridtsati tomakh*, vol. 25, Leningrad: Nauka; *Son smeshnogo cheloveka. Fantasticheskii rasskaz* (pp. 104–19).

Dostoevsky, F.M., 1994, *Son smeshnogo cheloveka / The Dream of a Ridiculous Man*, ed. W.J. Leatherbarrow, London: Bristol Classical Press.

Dostoevsky, Fyodor, 1968, *Great Short Works of Fyodor Dostoevsky*, New York: Harper & Row; *The Dream of a Ridiculous Man*, trans. David Magarshack (pp. 715–38).

Dostoevsky, Fyodor, *The Karamazov Brothers*, 1994, trans. Ignat Avsey, Oxford: Oxford University Press.

Fetzer, Leland, ed. and trans., 1982, *Pre-Revolutionary Russian Science Fiction: An Anthology (Seven Utopias and a Dream)*, Ann Arbor: Ardis.

Hodgson, William Hope, 1988, *The House on the Borderland*, London: Robinson Publishing.

Krzhizhanovsky, Sigizmund, 2006, *Seven Stories*, trans. Joanne Turnbull, Moscow: Glas.

Maiakovsky, V.V., 1995–61, *Polnoe sobranie sochinenii v trinadtsati tomakh*, Moscow: Gos. izd. Khudozhestvennoi literatury; *Chelovek*, vol. I, 1955 (pp. 243–72); *Pro eto*, vol. IV, 1957 (pp. 135–84).

[Medvedev] *Biblioteka russkoi fantastiki. 6 tom: Kosmorama*, Moscow: Russkaia kniga, 1997; *Zhivoi mertvets* (pp. 176–99); *4338-i god* (pp. 282–312).

Odoevsky, V.F., 1959, *Povesti i rasskazy*, Moscow: Gos. izdat; *Zhivoi mertvets* (pp. 306–31); *4338-i god* (pp. 416–48).

Odoevsky, V.F., 1982, *Poslednii kvartet Betkhovena*, Moscow: Moskovskii rabochii; *Zhivoi mertvets* (pp. 216–40); *4338-i god* (pp. 271–302).
Odoevsky, Vladimir, 1992, *The Salamander and Other Gothic Tales*, trans. Neil Cornwell, London: Bristol Classical Press; *The Live Corpse* (pp. 66–88).
Pamuk, Orhan, 2002, *My Name is Red* (*Benim Adim Kirmizi*, 1998), trans. Erdağ M. Göknar, London: Faber.
Stapledon, Olaf, 1988, *Star Maker*, Harmondsworth: Penguin.

Secondary sources

Aldiss, Brian W. with David Wingrove, *Trillion Year Spree: The History of Science Fiction*, London: Victor Gollancz, 1986.
Ashley, Mike, 1997, 'Hodgson, William Hope (1877–1918)', in *The Encyclopedia of Fantasy*, ed. John Clute and John Grant, London: Orbit, pp. 471–2.
Boulter, Amanda, 1993, '*The House on the Borderland*: the Sexual Politics of Fear', in *Creepers: British Horror and Fantasy in the Twentieth Century*, ed. Clive Bloom, London: Pluto Press, pp. 24–34.
Cornwell, Neil, 1986, *The Life, Times and Milieu of V.F. Odoyevsky, 1804–1869*, London: The Athlone Press.
Cornwell, Neil, 1998, *Vladimir Odoevsky and Romantic Poetics*, Providence and Oxford: Berghahn Books.
Crossley, Robert, 1994, *Olaf Stapledon: Speaking for the Future*, Liverpool: Liverpool University Press.
Suvin, Darko, 1979, *Metamorphoses of Science Fiction*, New Haven and London: Yale Univerity Press.

3

Seerman: the rise of the psychic detective

In his collection *Roots of Detection: The Art of Deduction before Sherlock Holmes* (1983), Bruce Cassiday provides illustrations of deductive thinking in a crime-solving context from as far back as Herodotus and *The Apocrypha*, and on into *The Arabian Nights*. Some commentators have called *Oedipus Rex* 'the first detective story' (see Sweeney in Merivale and Sweeney, 1999, 248). Cassiday then reaches relatively modern times, with Voltaire's *Zadig* and E.T.A. Hoffmann, before continuing through the nineteenth century, with names or works well known and lesser known. Other historians of detection also note Voltaire and add in Godwin's *Caleb Williams* (Binyon, 1990; Knight, 2004) and Charles Brockden Brown's *Wieland* (Knight, 2004). The point in these examples is very much logical deduction, or reasoning from objective evidence (Cassiday, 1983, 2).[1] Poe's three Auguste Dupin stories are the universally acknowledged epitome of this trend, soon more or less taken up by Dickens and Wilkie Collins in England, and by a number of writers in France: Cassiday offers samples from Eugène François Vidocq (who in fact precedes Poe), Alexandre Dumas and Émile Gaboriau's *Monsieur Lecoq*.[2]

Detection existed before Poe in English popular fiction, in the 'criminal broadsides' and the 'criminography' in the press of the early nineteenth century, as Heather Worthington (2005) has shown. Crime, without much detection, had been the mainstay of the *Newgate Calendar* in the eighteenth century, operating 'in a world drenched in Christian belief' (Knight, 2004, 4). Its glamorisation proceeded, thanks not least to the efforts of Thomas De Quincey – himself to be considered 'an authorial proto-detective' (Worthington, 2005, 27).[3] Logical, or artful, deduction is in any case one thing – with the birth of the amateur sleuth leading to Sherlock Holmes and to the gamut of twentieth-century police detectives and private eyes.[4] Psychic detection, however, is something rather different.

Certain pointers in this direction are to be found, even before Hoffmann, within European Gothic, in Schiller's unfinished novel *The Ghost-seer* (*Der Geisterseher*, 1798). A Swedenborgian type of paranormal and possible elaborate hoax, as well as crime, are certainly to be found in this key Gothic work, but, as Knight observes (2004, 19) – and as usual in these early works – 'there is very little actual detection involved'. However, Andrew Brown can still write of Schiller's Prince of ** 'in "detective" mode (in Book One), availing himself of the straightforward austerities of logical deduction and scientific methodology' (Schiller, 2003, xvii) in his efforts to comprehend the mysterious 'Russian' (or 'Armenian') dubbed '*The Unfathomable*' (ibid., 31).[5]

Hoffmann, master of the supernatural mystery tale of keen psychological (or proto-psychoanalytical) awareness, well recognised – not least by Freud himself – as anticipatory of Freud, might have seemed a likely candidate for the title of instigator of the story of psychic detection. But this is not in fact quite the case. Just as Poe's three tales of ratiocination, or Dupin detection (of 1841–4), mark a solitary phase in his *oeuvre*, before a return to something more like the ghostly horrific, Hoffmann's *Mademoiselle de Scudéri* (1819) stands alone in its author's work as a historical detective novella. Moreover, the Parisian crimes here are not solved by means of deduction (even through the good offices of a late seventeenth-century French anticipation of Miss Marple); still less are they solved by psychic insight. They are solved rather, as Andrew Brown affirms, 'by a series of unusually contingent chance events and hunches' (Hoffmann, 2002, xv); plus confession, also induced by chance past events. Whether for atmospheric purposes, or as mere traces of Hoffmannian motifs from elsewhere, phrases such as 'crazy ghost-seer' (17), reference to alchemy and the philosopher's stone, and possible diabolic influence are bandied about in a story seen (in contrast with the epistemological optimism of most detective fiction – an ethical pessimism notwithstanding) as 'doubly negative in its conclusions' and imbued with an 'ultimate pessimism' (xv, xviii).

Chevalier C. Auguste Dupin, the aristocratic private sleuth and master of deduction or, as he himself stresses, of 'analysis' in Poe's trio of pioneering detective tales, is ever keen to expatiate on his methods to (or through) his friend and confidant – our narrator, a kind of proto-Watson figure. Motive can sometimes be but a 'blundering idea' and coincidences happen all the time, 'without attracting even momentary notice'. Moreover, '[c]oincidences in general are great stumbling blocks in the way of that class of thinkers who have been educated to know nothing of the theory of probabilities' (*Rue Morgue*: Poe, 1966, 19). Coincidences, indeed, may startle even 'the calmest thinkers . . . into a vague yet thrilling half-credence in the supernatural' (*Marie Rogêt*: ibid., 27). Dupin speaks thus 'of coincidences and *no more*' (emphasis in the original), having 'no faith in praeternature' (ibid., 62).

There is, however, such a concept as 'the doctrine of chance' or 'the Calculus of Probabilities' (28). Evidence, observation (or the assessment from a distance of the observations and press publications of others in *The Mystery of Marie Rogêt*) and methodical procedure are of the essence; pains must be taken not 'to deflect from the line of ordinary analysis' (47). Even keener mental vigour may be required for analysis in a case immediately to hand, as in *The Purloined Letter*. However, a certain psychology must be added to rationalism, the quality of the poet to that of the mathematician. The value of being 'lucky', Dupin agrees, lies in 'an identification of the reasoner's intellect with that of his opponent' – in this case, the Minister D- (*The Purloined Letter*: Poe, 1966, 132). 'The principle of the *vis inertiae*', what is more, 'seems to be identical in physics and metaphysics' (135). According to Todorov (in his essay 'The Limits of Edgar Poe'), 'Dupin, a puppet-character lacking all "psychology" in the novelistic sense, offers lucid formulations of the laws of human psychic life' (Todorov, 1991, 100).

Following his inductive success in solving the murders in the Rue Morgue, in his own (up to that point) unexplained fashion, Dupin has ceased to be an obscure and purely private investigator. He has acquired 'the credit of intuition' and 'found himself the cynosure of the policial eyes' (*Marie Rogêt*: Poe, 1966, 28). No Dupin figure appears in Poe's slightly earlier story 'The Man of the Crowd' (1840); nevertheless, it is seen by Patricia Merivale as 'the first metaphysical gumshoe story' (Merivale and Sweeney, 1999, 104; see also 12–13 and 104–12 on that work).

Another fictional genre with a similarly long pedigree is the ghost story. Julia Briggs plots its history from ancient literatures to the nineteenth century in the first chapter, subtitled 'the Ghost Story from Lucian to Le Fanu', of her study *Night Visitors* (1977), noting the inset ghost stories in Petronius and Apuleius, and whisking spectrally through to Chaucer and Shakespeare, and on to Defoe and Scott.[6] Given the customary brevity of the horror tale, however, she comfortingly affirms that 'there is no danger of confusing the bare scaffolding of the ghost story with the rambling mansion of the Gothic novel' (Briggs, 1977, 13). Such 'scaffoldings' were to be found in *Blackwood's Edinburgh Magazine*, in such items as 'The Buried Alive' by John Galt (1821), which throws together premature burial, bodysnatching and 'galvanic experiment', and 'Le Revenant' (1827), by an otherwise unknown Henry Thomson, in which the narrator has survived a hanging (see Morrison and Baldick, 1995, 35–8, 73–87; their selection is taken from the years 1817 to 1832).[7]

At almost the same time, another Thomson – one Richard Thomson (writing as 'Anon.') – published his *Tales of an Antiquary* (in three volumes, 1828). The third volume seems to come closer to the present mark, in that it features the activities of a 'judicial astrologer' named Ptolemy Horoscope (who may derive from William Blake's astrologer friend John Varley), accompanied by an unreliable assistant called Titus Parable.[8] However, there is perhaps only one story ('The Cock Lane Ghost: A Legend of Snow Hill') in which a crime, in the strict sense (involving 'supernatural' events, and modelled on the Cock Lane case of 1762) is investigated.[9]

If the psychic detective is not to be located in earlier writings, one might expect such an entity to emerge as something of a fusion between the exponent of deduction and the seeker (or endurer) of the paranormal. We have noted already that the two principal founders of the modern detective story, Hoffmann and Poe, are rather better known for their (more typical) excursions into the supernatural (Poe's horror, indeed, was partly inspired by tales from *Blackwood's*: see Morrison and Baldick, 1995, *passim*). It would therefore not come as a great surprise, should those who really were the nineteenth-century pioneers of the psychic type of detective turn out also to have been writers of ghostly and horror fiction.

Before proceeding further, however, we should perhaps pause briefly, to note certain concepts introduced into narrative studies that may be worth keeping in mind as we approach such pioneering works or figures. The first is Todorov's notion of the fantastic (in his study *The Fantastic*: Todorov, 1973; French original first published 1970), depending on the reader's hesitation between a natural and a supernatural explanation of the events presented in a narrative. The fantastic is maintained when this question cannot be resolved. An eventual stimulus into the realms of the preternatural would push the work into the category of the 'marvellous'. Alternatively, if a resolution of such hesitation is tipped back into the natural world, then the work is said to fall under the designation of 'the uncanny' (at the more unlikely extreme of 'realism').[10]

It is at or around the borders between the fantastic and the marvellous, or the fantastic and the uncanny, that the putative psychic detective may seem most likely to lurk. The deductive analyst, while hinting at, usually only to deny, incursions of the marvellous, will remain within the confines of the natural, or of realism – albeit perhaps of uncanny-realism. Any such stress on the uncanny brings to mind, of course, Freud's influential essay 'The "Uncanny" ' (the original first published in 1919), ostensibly at least a study of Hoffmann's tale *The Sandman*. It also invites a consideration of reflections inspired by Freud's essay, a prominent recent example of which is Nicholas Royle's book *The uncanny* (2003).

Royle, in post-Todorovian (as well as post-Freudian) revisionist mode, sees the uncanny not as a literary genre (Royle, 2003, 19), but 'a reading-effect', reminding us too of the mixed-genre form of *The Sandman* (ibid., 44). In his chapter discussing what he calls the 'telepathy effect' of the narrative text (256–76), he seeks to supplant 'omniscience' (and such related narratological terms as 'point of view' and 'focalization') with 'telepathy' – a term which, as he says, only entered the vocabulary in the late nineteenth century (260–1). The emergence then of 'telepathy', Royle considers, 'figures an important moment in what we have called the disappearance of omniscience, as well as in the origins of psychoanalysis'; telepathy 'calls for a quite different kind of critical storytelling than that promoted by the religious, panoptical delusion of omniscience' (261). He writes of 'phantom communications' and 'unconscious, absent or ghostly emotions' (268), of telepathy 'as a *literary phenomenon*' (his emphasis) and 'a concept and effect intimately bound up with writing and death, the spectral and unprogrammable' (272). Detection as such does not make an appearance in his analysis, but the two nineteenth-century examples he does cite are George Eliot's *The Lifted Veil* (1859) and Dickens's *The Mystery of Edwin Drood* (1870).

While he does discuss works by Poe (featuring doubles and premature burial), Royle does not, then, broach the detection stories. Near the beginning of the first of these, however, Dupin is thought by the narrator to have 'been enabled to fathom [his] soul' (in the matter of the minor character named Chantilly) – without, of course, using the word 'telepathy' (*Rue Morgue*: Poe, 1966, 6). Wholesale acceptance of Royle's telepathic approach to narratology in modern and postmodernist fiction might necessitate an ambitious step; an intuition as to its usefulness in connection with the more psychological, psychoanalytical and psychic figures and texts of detective fiction, however, could be another matter.

*   *   *   *   *

Vladimir Odoevsky's 'dilogy' (or 'double-novella') *The Salamander* (*Salamandra*) was first published in 1841 (in two separate parts under the titles 'The Southern Shore of Finland at the Beginning of the Eighteenth Century' and 'The Salamander'). It was combined, under the second title (the second part being then renamed 'Elsa'), in 1844. The bipartite 'dilogy' structure comprises a genuine continuation in narrative terms, while signalling a radical break in the work as regards narrational mode, chronological leap and generic emphasis. The first part, as its title indicates, is a historical tale, concerned with Russo-Finnish relations and imbued with Finnish folklore (largely from *The Kalevala*). While the second part, 'Elsa', continues these themes through the Finnish characters Yakko and Elsa, who have moved from St Petersburg to Moscow following the death of Peter the Great (and a consequent severe dip in

Yakko's fortunes), it is rather more dominated by occult motifs and a Gothic atmosphere. Discussion of *The Salamander* has hitherto concentrated on the work as an example of colonial-imperial Gothic (Cornwell, 2003), or on the theme of engendering and the figure of Elsa (Ramsey, 1999).

For present purposes, our interest is in the second part, and in particular in the person of the secondary narrator (the primary narrator's uncle). This character's lack of a name (being referred to just as 'uncle') has not, of course, helped in identifying him – let alone establishing him – as an early figure in the development of the psychic detective. Cynthia Ramsey, in a footnote, refers to Uncle (as we shall call him) as 'a double of Faust from *Russian Nights* [*Russkie nochi*] and Odoevskii himself', serving as 'the cultural translator between the "folk" and the "rational"'' (Ramsey, 1999, 164, n. 26). Odoevsky was fond of creating older *alter ego* figures. In addition to Faust, the link man in his philosophical frame-tale novel (first integral publication 1844), we can also point to Iriney Modestovich Gomozeyko, the 'collector' of tales featured in the *Variegated Tales* cycle (*Pestrye skazki*, 1833), who had been intended to play a larger part in Odoevsky's subsequent works. In the event the only return appearance Gomozeyko makes in a finished work is as the garrulous storyteller of 'The Ghost' (or 'The Apparition': *Prividenie*, 1838). Gomozeyko is a very similar figure to Uncle, having been introduced as 'Master of Philosophy and member of various learned societies'; he is an afficionado of occult sciences, who knows 'all possible languages: living, dead and half-dead' and just about everything else – a poverty-stricken encyclopedist (see Cornwell, 1986, p. 45).

One of Gomozeyko's *Variegated Tales* (entitled 'The Tale of a Dead Body, Belonging to No One Knows Whom': included in Odoevsky, 1992, 17–25) does contain certain elements of the detective story (discussed by Sucur, 2001, 142–5). It is also a tale that could almost have been written to anticipate (by well over half a century) Henry James's remarks (in his New York preface to *The Aspern Papers*): 'Recorded and attested "ghosts" are . . . as little expressive, as little dramatic, above all as little continuous and conscious and responsive, as is consistent with their taking the trouble – and an immense trouble they find it, we gather – to appear at all' (quoted by Briggs, 1977, 63–4).

Another story by Odoevsky, known as 'Letter IV [to Countess Ye P. Rostopchina]' (see Odoevsky, 1992, 60–5), is notable as an early example of the 'locked room' type of mystery, as well as for featuring the Count Saint-Germain, a legendary but historical figure. Saint-Germain had been used slightly earlier by Pushkin in his Gothic masterpiece *The Queen of Spades* (1833) and, much more recently, he has resurfaced in Umberto Eco's occult extravaganza, *Foucault's Pendulum* (1988) and elsewhere.[11]

Original drafts for *The Salamander* had indicated a tale of alchemy set in medieval Europe, involving the Inquisition. Such a Gothic theme, pursuing a Faustian alchemical quest, blurs into lost primitive sorcery (here represented by the Finns), projecting the reader forward in its second part to a Moscow ghost story of the 1830s, in which echoes of an imperial past may be coming home to roost. Yakko, moving to Moscow, has taken a kind of revenge for the loss of his glittering Petrine career, but the ultimate retribution is wreaked – on Russian society and on him – by the eponymous Elsa (his love-torn purported sibling-salamander).

The impersonal third-person narrative of the first part gives way, then, in 'Elsa' to a first-person discourse, operating in the present of the 1830s in Moscow. This unnamed narrator yields to an embedded narrative stemming from his Uncle – the 'explanation' of strange phenomena heard and observed (by Uncle and nephew) in a Moscow boyar's house, and reproduced 'as far as my [i.e., the nephew's] memory permits, . . . in full' (Odoevsky, 1992, 187). Uncle's tale (if that is what it is, although it clearly requires a knowledge of the events of the first part of the dilogy) may have been expounded as a provocation to his sceptical nephew. The apparent hauntings (howling, groaning and an apparition) which are indeed witnessed by the pair at the boyar's house have been accompanied by a sparring bout between 'nine-teenth-century logic' (ibid., 183), or the scientific rationalist approach (the nephew), and at the very least an openness to mystery and ancient knowledge (Uncle). 'The poor wretches!', Uncle admonishes the haunters: 'when are you going to pay off your debt for this?' (186).

The Moscow events of over a century before (in Uncle's explanation) centre largely on obsessive alchemical pur-suits, carried out by Yakko, together with an ageing count, aided by Elsa – operating both in real life and as salamander within the alchemists' stove. What ensues is the discovery of a valuable dye (if not of gold) and an elixir of life, in conjunction with such occult phenomena as spontaneous human combustion (a good decade before Dickens was to employ it in *Bleak House*), body-switching and supernatural arson. Other opinions – hearsay, criminality, madness (real or feigned) – are mooted at the end, and the nephew pur-ports still a preference for a verdict of 'invention', 'joke' and 'phantasmagoria', 'hopeful that every reasonable reader will agree with [him] on this' (212). The Moscow house had been built (by the late prince, an old-time acquaintance of the youthful Uncle) on a smouldering ruin, the site of Yakko's alleged antics.

The alternative solutions offered at the end, together with the nephew's coy attitude, allow *The Salamander* to remain within the category of the fantastic. Explanations may be uncanny, or they may be marvellous: textually this is unde-cidable. Yakko and Elsa have, at times at least, a telepathic relationship ('interjected the Salamander, having read his thoughts': 206) – to say nothing of the nephew's verbatim reproduction of Uncle's narrative. Uncle himself, if perhaps not quite a psychic detective, is at least an active exponent of ghost-busting fieldwork (or rather, floor work). He is, as a constant follower of 'the wondrous path of knowledge' (177), particularly in its mystical aspects, at very least, a figure pointing in the direction of the 'psychic doctor'.

*   *   *   *   *

According to Julia Briggs (1977, 54), it is 'the gap between what actually happens and its scientific cause which distinguishes the ghost story from science fiction'. And it is in the years between the heyday of the ghost story and the serious rise of science fiction, or equally between the spread of Mesmerism and the emergence of psychoanalysis, that we may expect to come upon the psychic doctor. Worthington (2005, 30) points up the parallel professional development in this period of medicine and criminology, producing 'that invaluable tool of detection, forensic medicine'. One writer who graduated from the promulgation of medical to legal 'reminiscences' was the once-popular Samuel Warren (1807–77).[12] Such an emergent figure may soon be poised to evolve into something in the nature of the psychic detective. This would prove to be particularly so later in the century, in the years following the birth of the Society for Psychical Research (1882) – an event which gave rise, only then, to the introduction of the term 'telepathy' (*OED*: for a full study of the 'invention' of this notion, see Luckhurst, 2002).[13] The word, according to Luckhurst (2002, 203), apparently entered the general language only in the 1930s.

Early works by Edward Bulwer-Lytton are noted by various commentators (see Knight, 2004 and Worthington, 2005); a murder investigation, excerpted from *Pelham* (1828), is included in Cassiday's collection (1983, 67–81). Bulwer-Lytton's novel *Paul Clifford* (1830) looked into the responsibilities for criminality. We shall look at two of his later works shortly. Early detective writing, whether avowedly fictional or supposedly memoiristic, may not, then, really be expected to display psychic qualities. However, William Russell (described as a 'hack journalist' by Worthington, 2005, 129), posing as one 'Waters' in his *Recollections of a Detective Police Officer* (published serially 1849–53; collected 1856) can include a case he calls 'The Monomaniac', featuring an obsessive who imagines a widowed fellow-lodger to be 'his long-dead love returned' (Worthington, 2005, 146). Warren has a chilling story called 'The Spectre-Smitten' (Morrison and Baldick, 1995, 215–41). At the detective end, Inspector Bucket of *Bleak House* (1853) is considered to have methods (albeit in reality 'those of his predecessors') that are 'cloaked in a quasi-supernatural aura' (Worthington, 2005, 167).

In 1856 Wilkie Collins produced a collection called *After Dark*, presented in frame-tale form as 'a poor painter's stories which his wife has written down for him After Dark!' (Collins, 331). There is little formal detection (in the Dupin sense) in these stories, though *Sister Rose* (set somewhat Hoffmann-esquely in historical Paris, although a hundred years later) does sport a 'Chief Police Agent Lomaque' (serving under Robespierre), who can later fall back on his 'old police-officer practice' (ibid., 155). The spectre of 'The White Women' is evoked in *Gabriel's Marriage*: 'bright as lightning in the darkness, mighty as the angels in stature, sweeping like the wind over the sea, in their long white garments, with their white hair trailing far behind them!' They 'beckon awfully to the raging sea to give up its dead' (198). In the same story, criminal recollection can bring about 'the supernatural panic deformity' of a guilty face (228). Another phantasmic face is contrived through the dubious offices of Father Rocco – himself at times a 'spectral' figure (281) – in *The Yellow Mask* (set mainly in Pisa). What appears as 'the powers of the other world . . . interfering with mortals at masquerades' (295) turns out to be occasioned through the plaster cast procured from a statue of Minerva. Mystery and suspense, with a strong atmosphere of crime or malicious scheming, merge in these tales by Collins with speculation, confession and sentimentality.

Bulwer-Lytton's story *The Haunted and the Haunters; or, The House and the Brain* appeared anonymously in *Blackwood's* in 1859. The narrator feels moved to investigate a haunted house in London, in which an open-ended variety of terrifying spectral, and some physical, manifestations occur. A part of the dwelling and its previous inhabitants prove to have a pre-history of malicious events (not unlike Odoevsky's Moscow house in *The Salamander*), with a curse having been placed on the house and 'the dwellers therein' (Bulwer-Lytton, 2000, 159). In the narrator's view, 'the Supernatural is the Impossible' and apparitions must be explainable by some human agency – or at least in terms of an occult science, such as 'mesmeric influence' or 'electro-biology' (ibid., 146, 153), across some distance in space and time. This is a phenomenon that would later be called 'remote telepathy'.

The Haunted and the Haunters had an extra chapter, cut on reprinting, which Bulwer-Lytton used instead as a basis for his lengthy 'romance' *A Strange Story*, serialised in Dickens's magazine *All The Year Round* in 1861. Here we encounter a sequence of doctors, varyingly involved with – whether confronting or engaged in, attempting to practise or to explain away – psychic medicine, plus a welter of science, pseudo-science and occult proceedings. The narrator, Dr Allen Fenwick, an advocate of 'stern materialism' and 'common-sense' (ch. I), taking over the provincial English practice of the retiring and eminently sensible Dr Julius Faber, disparages the Mesmerism and somnambular clairvoyance of his 'rival' Dr Lloyd (who dies off almost immediately, parting from his repudiator with a death-bed curse) and of his ineffectual successor of similar mind, a Dr Jones.

This rich medical farrago becomes further and further embroiled in preternatural happenings, eastern mysticism and 'visitations from the Shadowland of ghosts and sorcerers' (ch. XLI) with the entry of the enchanting 'spoilt darling of Material Nature' (ch. LXXVI), and raiser of demons in his quest for immortality, named Margrave. Criminal actions ensue, plus a trance visited upon Fenwick's hyper-sensitive and receptive fiancée (later his mesmerised bride), Lilian. 'Detection', in the criminal sense, is purportedly accomplished by the true instigator of the transgressions (Margrave); in the intellectual – and transcendental – sense, it is endlessly discussed (particularly once the action has moved to expatriation in Australia) by Fenwick and his elderly mentor, Faber.[14] Margrave may be seen as something like a successful combination (at least over some decades) of Yakko and the Count from Odoevsky's *The Salamander*, equally obsessed with the elixir of life.[15] He is also, perhaps, a more gregarious variant of Schiller's 'Armenian'. Marie Roberts, in her study *Gothic Immortals*, reads Bulwer-Lytton's *Zanoni* and *A Strange Story* (on the latter work, see Roberts, 1990, 187–98) as 'Rosicrucian novels', designating Margrave therefore a 'false' aspirant to the persuasion of Rosicrucianism.

This 'strange' and rambling 'tale', although excessively permeated with theoretical digressions and philosophical footnotes, somehow retains until the end at least a degree of suspense. Mention (notably, if slightly anachronistically) is introduced of 'spirit manifestations' in America (ch. XLV), while the author (writing in 1861) again suffers from the then absence in the vocabulary of the word 'telepathy', in raising the question: 'Have certain organizations like that of Margrave the power to impress, through space, the imaginations of those over whom they have forced a control?' (ch. LXXIII).

Dickens had supplied *Bleak House* with Inspector Bucket and had published a series of 'Detective Police' anecdotes for his *Household Words* in the early 1850s (see Worthington, 2005, 158–69), as well as commissioning somewhat similar contributions to his periodicals from other writers. A little closer to psychic detection, however (and in contrast to Bulwer-Lytton's *A Strange Story*), is his highly condensed tale 'The Trial for Murder' (1865). Here the detection remains unexplained, taking place off-page (by detectives unknown), but the nameless narrator (in fact a London banker) undergoes 'presentiment' and 'vision', and appears to be accorded (for an instant at least) 'in some occult manner' (Dickens, 737) a power of telepathic touch.[16] Unexpectedly jury-summonsed and appointed 'Foreman of the Jury', the narrator sees the victim in the courtroom and during the juridical deliberations throughout the murder trial resulting from this mysteriously intuited case. (He is seemingly alone in this, though an apparition does fleetingly manifest itself more widely as a 'thirteenth' juror.) While not fully revealing itself to others involved, the 'Appearance' nevertheless, the narrator claims, 'could invisibly, dumbly, and darkly overshadow their minds' (ibid., 741). The murderer, moreover, when declared guilty, contends that he knew he was doomed, as '*the Foreman of my Jury . . . somehow got to my bedside in the night, woke me, and put a rope round my neck*' (743; italics in the original). In *The Trial for Murder*, the process of criminal detection is elided in favour of preternatural vision and intuition – or the phenomenon of the 'hunch' assuming a more psychic form.

A medical duo is met with again in Sheridan Le Fanu's collection, or cycle, of stories, *In a Glass Darkly* (1872), in the shape of Dr Martin Hesselius, a German physician with scientific interests in the widest sense, and the collector of mysterious 'cases'. The unnamed frame-tale narrator of the cycle, who presents a selection of Hesselian cases, is a non-practitioner, though 'carefully educated in medicine and surgery', 'an enthusiast' in the profession and Hesselius's long-term 'medical secretary' (Le Fanu, 1990, 3). Hesselius himself is only remotely active in the first of these case-tales, *Green Tea* (first published separately, in 1869), in which he relates the events known from his acquaintance with a certain 'Revd Mr Jennings', who, possibly through over-consumption of the eponymous beverage, undergoes visitations from a spectral monkey. The remaining cases comprise the narratives of others, retained by Hesselius with occasional comments from himself attached. The second of these, *The Familiar* (in fact published as a story much earlier, in 1851), is the narrative of another clergyman. This concerns a former naval commander suffering from the repeated hauntings of a man (seemingly reduced in size) whom he had caused to be ill treated and knows to have died years before in Naples. A third manuscript recounts the case of an eighteenth-century hanging-judge (the eponymous Mr Justice Harbottle), spectrally sentenced to hang himself. The volume is completed with two longer cases: *The Room in the Dragon Volant*, in which a young traveller is entrapped, by a woman and a drug (called *imago mortis*), in immediately post-Napoleonic France; and *Carmilla*, which combines (strikingly enough for its time) a strongly implicit lesbian sexuality with vampirism.

Hesselius, as the author of 'Essays on Metaphysical Medicine' (ibid., 7), holds ideas deriving from German Romantic philosophy with traces of Swedenborg. He has been duly noticed as a 'psychic doctor hero' (Briggs, 1977, 38), or as 'one of the first in a line of psychic doctors, or occult detectives' (Cornwell, 1990, 91). While he may indeed, at least potentially, be seen as something of an amalgam of the questing Dr Frankenstein and the analytical Auguste Dupin, he remains curiously unrealised and inactive. Not only does he not dominate the collection in the way we might expect; he in fact recedes steadily in prominence after the first tale, giving way to his 'editor' and then to subsidiary narrators. Even when an exorcist and vampire-slayer is called for, in 'Carmilla', the task is allotted not to Hesselius, but to a certain Baron Vordenburg, who is expressly brought in just for that purpose.

Yet, despite not satisfying certain aspects of its potential (such as an elaboration of the underlying tension between the convictions of clergymen and scientific doctors), *In a Glass Darkly* does achieve a curious, if fragmented, unity as a cycle. This is accomplished through thematic progression (from idiosyncratic spectral visitation to vampirism) and geographical expansion eastwards – from Ireland to Austria, or the Anglo-Irish to the mid-European. The title may be seen as a (biblical) misquotation – 'in' rather than 'through' a glass darkly (W.J. Mc Cormack, introduction: Le Fanu, 1990, xii) – but one that is surely intentional. Given that a number of the Hesselius notebook entries have purportedly been translated, the tales reach the reader through something of a linguistic glass, while 'Le Fanu's fiction contributes to a new psychic diversity', in which a range of 'old solidities' are in process of being 'dissolved and dispersed' (ibid., xiv).

*   *   *   *   *

Such a process gathers considerable steam by the 1890s. One Paul Cushing (a pseudonym for Roland Alexander Woodseys) had published a work called *Doctor Caesar Crowl – Mind Curer* in 1887. Luckhurst provides an assessment of this period in the introduction to his *Late Victorian Gothic Tales* anthology (2005); and in his 2002 monograph ('many authors associated with fin-de-siècle Gothic . . . produced texts saturated with possibilities lifted from psychical research': 185). The Society for Psychical Research was in full swing; a proportion of the Victorian English-set fiction of Henry James in this decade took the form of the ghost story (most famously *The Turn of the Screw*, 1898). A work which contained most of the ingredients of present interest, even if not combined in quite the form now sought or expected, was Arthur Machen's novella of fragmentary construction, *The Great God Pan* (1894: included in Luckhurst, 2005, 183–233). Featured here is an exponent of 'transcendental medicine' (one Dr Raymond), preternatural invocation, crimes and suicides, and an element of canny detection (conducted by one protagonist, Villiers). It may not have been essential for an aspirant to psychic detection to have received medical training as such, but with the various psychological developments taking place towards the end of the nineteenth century, it seems commonly to have been thought a great help.

J.-K. Huysmans, it has been suggested by Terry Hale, particularly with his novel *Là-Bas* (*The Damned*, 1891), although this was not translated into English until 1924, may also have left an almost 'immediate legacy' in the development of the 'distinctive subgenre within the detective story' of the psychic sleuth, particularly in the fiction of such writers as Machen, Blackwood and, a bit later, Aleister Crowley (Hale's Introduction to Huysmans, 2001, xxi). This would have come largely through the conversations of the main characters, and their references to the esoteric sources of 'Mysticism, Astrology and Alchemy, the three great sciences of the Middle Ages' (ibid., 116), rather than any real detection. There is, though, no shortage of horrific criminality, especially arising from researches into the career of the child-murderer Gilles de Rais, but with sufficient too in the 'modern' period. 'Conversations about matters other than religion or art are always trivial and vain', according to Durtal (176), and these frequently descend to the black arts. The second main character (Durtal's confidant, des Hermies) is a psychic doctor of sorts (another is an astrologer). Moreover, Huysmans – whose day-job was deputy chief clerk at the Sûreté Générale (or national criminal investigation bureau) – himself penned the manuscript of *The Damned* (along with the biographical pamphlet offshoot on Gilles de Rais) on 'the magnificent stationery of the Ministry of the Interior' (xii).

Bram Stoker's *Dracula* (1897), yet another work of a highly fragmented construction, revives the Anglo-Irish tendency for this genre of writing, picking up in particular on two features inherited via Le Fanu: the psychic doctor and vampirism. It also similarly spreads its setting eastwards, from south-western England (Exeter), plus Whitby and London, to Transylvania and Bulgaria (or rather, as with Count Dracula himself, the reverse – as the opening narrative comes from Jonathan Harker in Bistritz, Romania). Again, we have a pair of doctors: John Seward, who presides over a lunatic asylum, and the arch-vampire-slayer, Professor Abraham Van Helsing, from Amsterdam. Dr Seward, having formerly been Van Helsing's student, calls in his old guru at a time of crisis. Dr Van Helsing (as he is frequently called), combines many of the attributes of his predecessors, as 'a philosopher and a metaphysician' (Stoker, 1996, 112), and 'a professor of the healing craft' (ibid., 119); but he is also a lawyer (163). More specifically, Van Helsing – according anyway to the 'lunatic' Renfield (who at certain times seems to know what he is talking about) – had 'revolutionised therapeutics by his discovery of the continuous evolution of brain-matter' (244).

Van Helsing, according to Harker (188), 'is the man to unmask [Dracula] and hunt him out'. 'I have clues which we can follow', Van Helsing indeed obligingly volunteers, 'in our great quest' (217, 218). He has also evolved a 'philosophy of crime', according to which the true criminal (a status to which Dracula has by now been reduced) 'is predestinate to crime', is 'clever and cunning and resourceful' – empirically single-minded, but 'of child-brain in much' (341).[17] Van Helsing has studied 'the powers of the Un-Dead' (or *nosferatu*), through 'the lore and experience of the ancients' (214), and indeed 'all the papers relating to this monster' (301), largely through the researches of his alchemist friend, one 'Arminius of Buda Pesth' (302). Well equipped intellectually as Van Helsing may thus be to supervise (and finalise) the hunting down of Dracula, most of the empirical detective work is in the event performed by the other members of his 'team' (later frequently referred to as 'the Crew of Light'). Important thinking is undertaken too by Mina Harker – in addition to the vital information she supplies under hypnosis and by means of remote (vampiric) telepathy, serving as what Luckhurst (2002, 212) terms 'an occult telephone'.

A strange 'doubling' quality emerges between Van Helsing and Count Dracula, as, within a generic context too of the fantastic, the former combats his adversary through an amalgam of pagan methodology and a revived drenching (for opponent and reader alike) in Christian belief and ritual. Alchemy is brought to bear against shape-shifting and supposed diabolic influence. Irritating as Van Helsing's pontifications in his inconsistently punctured English may be (as well as other features of Stoker's narratives: see Maud Ellmann's introduction to *Dracula* in Stoker, 1996), he has to be acknowledged as the first fully fledged and genuinely active psychic doctor-cum-detective.[18]

Algernon Blackwood's Dr John Silence appeared, in a collection published in 1908, as an overtly proclaimed psychic doctor – being 'known more or less generally as the "Psychic Doctor"' (Blackwood, 1997, 2), or even, in the narrative of Hubbard, his devoted assistant, or secretary, 'the great psychic doctor' (ibid., 203), and 'a true diviner of souls' (209).[19] The 'eccentric' Silence, 'rich by accident, and by choice – a doctor', works only 'free-lance', taking 'cases that interested him for some special reason' (1–2). Nevertheless, he still has a reception room with 'padded walls' (231) and is ready to use 'a soothing and persuasive narcotic' (232) on troublesome 'patients'. Known for his 'knowledge of occultism' ('"Oh please, that dreadful word!" he interrupted'), his 'wonderful clairvoyant gift' and 'trained psychic knowledge' (1), Silence puts 'all perception' (clairvoyance included) down to 'the result of vibrations' and sensitivity thereto (9).[20] 'I have yet to come across a problem that is not natural', he declares, 'and has not a natural explanation' (102). This approach still allows, however, for the influence of 'Dark Powers', the 'old life', paganism, 'old Finnish magic' or Egyptian gods, alchemy, the 'astral body', witchcraft and reincarnation – as well as the effects of drugs, synaesthesia, telepathy, a fourth dimension, or even lycanthropy.

John Silence, in his chosen cases (or, at least, in the six of them which reach us), has to combat dark forces presented not so much in traditional ghost-story terms as in what William Hughes (2005) terms 'a discourse characteristic of the investigative occultism of the later-Victorian and Edwardian periods' (post-1882, and the advent of the Society for Psychical Research). In effect the psychic doctor may be seen as 'the *zeitgeist* of a speculative age', functioning as 'the bridge between portrayed secular and spiritual disciplines' (ibid.). As in earlier stories contributing to this tradition, Christian sentiments do get expressed, and one clergyman does feature (in *The Camp of the Dog*). However, this hapless individual, the Reverend Timothy Maloney, has switched from the church to tutoring; in any case, 'bullied as a young man into a lucrative family living, he had in turn bullied his mind into some semblance of orthodox beliefs' (Blackwood, 1997, 174). Before the saga is through, Maloney is ready 'to shoot first – and pray afterwards!' (ibid., 220). Silence's occasionally active cohort, and in some of the cases a Watson-like narrator, Mr Hubbard, is neither a medical officer nor a churchman; there is perhaps a hint, though, that he may have been an Egyptologist (see 138).

Silence's own role in the related proceedings can vary from merely that of the listener, as in *Ancient Sorceries*, to his crucial intervention, in particular in *Secret Worship*. In the latter story, the protagonist, one Harris, revisits his old school in Germany (modelled seemingly on one attended there by Blackwood himself), only to find that it has (it would seem literally, as well as spiritually) gone to hell. The opening Silence story, *A Psychical Invasion*, is reminiscent of earlier works noted above (by Bulwer-Lytton, whom Blackwood would have known, and Odoevsky, whom he could not). The eponymous invasion stems from 'a woman of singularly atrocious life and character', hanged in 1798, who operated from a large old house, standing on the sight of the haunted one now under investigation, and who – incidentally – 'availed herself of the resources of the lower magic to attain her ends' (42). Dr Silence's 'secretary' had unearthed the details 'from the records of the Newgate Calendar' (43).

If Silence's opponents generally seem to come from 'another region' (the past, near or distant, 'galvanised into active life again by the will of a trained manipulator': ibid.), there is one story in which, it is noted, 'Silence is . . . revealed in more of a detecting role than usual' (Briggs, 1977, 63). This is *The Nemesis of Fire*, in which *The Egyptian Book of the Dead* offers answers for dealing with 'a fire-elemental' released as a result of common theft – first (though, in good colonial terms, taken less seriously) of a mummy from Egypt. Mainly, however, the troubles arise from further interference with the said mummy, in the shape of a 'sacred scarabaeus' (142) stolen by the original finder's sister. Silence's detective work deals effectively here equally with the ancient preternatural intervention and the living criminal.

William Hope Hodgson's protagonist Carnacki came upon the scene in the collection *Carnacki the Ghost-Finder*, published in 1913. As Briggs (1977, 63) has noted, Carnacki brings to bear upon his psychic endeavours more of 'a practical approach to the occult' than is to be found among his predecessors.[21] This includes the innovative application of modern technology. In addition to chalked pentacles and circles, garlic and a traditional range of expendable animals, Carnacki constructs an Electric Pentacle and uses flashlight photography, as well as a primitive phonograph and a process with a ribbon, appearing to anticipate the tape recorder, so that 'I was even then hearing "mentally" by means of his effort of memory' – in a kind of mechanised telepathy (Hodgson, 1980, 202). In the view of Binyon (1990, 13), Carnacki 'is unique among fictional detectives, . . . in that he concerns himself solely with occult phenomena'.

That being as it may, Carnacki has plenty of theories, but he does not know everything. He is far more consistently active than his predecessors, frequently putting life and soul at risk, and alternating between emotional states of 'funk' and 'pluck'. He uses hypnotic suggestion, but he can also acknowledge 'deduction' (Hodgson, 1980, 158). There is a considerably greater element of detection in Carnacki's cases; indeed, five of the nine stories resolve themselves either totally or partly through fraudulent or criminal explanations. 'Induced haunting', the 'ab-human' or the influence or appearance of Monstrosities from the 'Outer Circle' – 'emanations' from gas belts circling the Earth (of which 'the Outer Circle is the psychic circle': 237) – may provide the other causes. Vibrations are liable to be of (or from) the essence. Supposedly haunted houses, with of course a history, are the usual setting (in two cases in the West of Ireland – one being put down by the local police as disguising the antics 'of a certain "political" club': 81); one story features a haunted ship.[22]

One of the quirks of *Carnacki the Ghost-Finder* lies in the protagonist's personality, combined with the repeated form of narrative presentation. Carnacki always invites a tame quartet of devoted adherents to dinner, and then regales them with a monologue on a chosen case (whether in progress, or recent, or recalled for interest's sake). He then dispatches them into the London air with the 'genial' and 'recognised formula': 'Out you go!' There is no argument, rarely an interruption, with usually a couple of questions tolerated at the end. The proceedings are recorded by a Watson-like frame narrator (named just twice – as 'Dodgson'), who otherwise has no involvement. His own occupation is unclear, although another of the quartet, Arkright, is said by Carnacki to have 'dipped deeper into the science of magic' than he has himself: 175).

Carnacki uses, then, a combination of pseudo-scientific theorising and technology and lashings of occult mumbo-jumbo (the 'Sigsand MS.' and the 'Saaamaaa ritual') to combat the 'Outer Monstrosities', which may manifest themselves as a materialising hand or a gigantic hog. Both from content and narrative tone, it is difficult to know how serious Hodgson (or, for that matter, Dodgson) is. A tongue-in-cheek quality may well be appearing to gather pace – especially towards the end of the collection with the story 'The Hog' – with his mingling of wry humour together with a perhaps genuinely terrified obsession. Forgotten for a number of years after his death in action in 1918, Hodgson was revived by H.P. Lovecraft and admired by Dennis Wheatley (who used a 'Sussamma Ritual' in his *The Devil Rides Out*, 1935).

The 'great beast' of occultism, Aleister Crowley (under the pseudonym of Edward Kelly), tried his hand at a kind of

Taoist psychic fiction with a series of (pro-German) stories published in a New York periodical (*The International*) in 1917–18, relatively recently collected as *The Scrutinies of Simon Iff*.[23] Worthy, perhaps, of at least brief mention as a successor to the figures of Silence and Carnacki is Sax Rohmer's psychic investigative protagonist, Moris Klaw, in *The Dream Detective* – a figure of 'compendious occult knowledge', who described himself as a 'humble explorer of the etheric borderland' and recipient of 'psychic photographs' (Luckhurst, 2002, 188).[24] Incidentally, as noted by Binyon (1990, 127), Rohmer was also the creator of the sinister oriental villain, Dr Fu Manchu. The prime emerging populariser of detective fiction, Agatha Christie, also tried her hand for a while at psychic detection, through the person of a certain Mr Harley Quin.[25]

*   *   *   *   *

If, no sooner did he develop into 'maturity', the psychic detective tipped over into a form of modernist parody, then, given his origins in Gothic and early Romantic fiction, that might be a fitting culmination.[26] The detective story itself had been experiencing such treatment over the period from the later decades of the nineteenth century. Back in the 1880s in Russia, Chekhov was responding to the cult of Gaboriau by means of pastiche. In his story *The Swedish Match* (*Shvedskaia spichka*, 1883), he conducts this operation largely through parodic plotting, introducing a murder victim who turns out to be alive (see Claire Whitehead's analysis, 2005). One might also suspect something of a pastiche of Dostoevsky's psychological sleuth from *Crime and Punishment*, Porfiry Petrovich.[27] Chekhov follows this, publishing in 1884–85 what is often considered to be his only novel, *The Shooting Party* (*Drama na okhote*) – probably the first detective story in which the investigating narrator turns out to be the murderer (see Rayfield, 1999, 22–4). His one psychic story, *The Black Monk* (*Chernyi monakh*, 1894), in which the legend of a black monk manifests itself, by mirage through time and space, to an increasingly demented academic, does not involve criminal investigation.[28] Unfortunately Chekhov, himself a medical doctor, never produced a work combining these elements.

Sherlock Holmes must, of course, be said to have been the dominant detective figure over his published career (stretching from 1887 to 1927), if not beyond. Indeed, according to Knight (2004, 55), 'Doyle's creation is unquestionably an apotheosis, a conveying of quasi-divine status on the figure that had slowly emerged through the nineteenth century'. Carnacki might in part be parodying Holmes, shooting off into supposedly psychic realms, to regale his cohorts with reports of his antics and references to multiple other cases. By a similar token, and by the 1920s, Doyle too may have been sending himself up a modicum – along with such psychic investigative pseudo-brethren of Holmes as Van Helsing, Silence and Carnacki. This may anyway seem a plausible reading at least of the late story *The Sussex Vampire* (1924: see Doyle, 1953, 1178–96).

Holmes, reminiscing on a number of cases, recorded or unrecorded, when called to a case of supposed vampirism snarls at his 'great index volume', mentioning the phenomenon in Hungary and Transylvania: 'Rubbish, Watson, rubbish! What have we to do with walking corpses who can only be held in their grave by stakes driven through their hearts? It's pure lunacy'. Some other means of blood sucking may be a different matter, but 'No ghosts need apply' (ibid., 1179). Holmes, thanks to 'my scientific methods' (1187) – 'exaggerated' as these may be by Watson – presumes to have solved the problem, through the preliminary interview with his distressed client, before even setting foot in the afflicted straggling Sussex house. Indeed, the administering of a South American poison (and consequent need for its oral extraction) duly turns out to have been the cause. 'The idea of a vampire was to me absurd', Holmes emphatically declares: 'Such things do not happen in criminal practice in England' (1194).

* * * * *

If the psychic detective, in the sense traced here, disappeared into a morass of parody, or was launched off into the realms of horror or science fiction (leading towards Buffy the vampire slayer and her 'watchers'[29]), what happened more generally to the figure of the detective? The ages of alchemy, Galvanism and Mesmerism, followed by the era of Psychical Research (even if the latter may never quite conclude), gave way to that of psychoanalysis (long after Freud and the 'uncanny', Poe was to be dissected by Lacan and Derrida). Such subgeneric developments as 'the psychothriller' (see Knight, 2004, 146–52) were bound to lie ahead. The paths of the police detective and the private eye have been outlined in standard surveys of detective fiction (those cited here and a number of others). R. Austin Freeman's protagonist Dr John Thorndyke ('the archetype of forensic experts': Knight, 2004, 69), conceived as a rival to Holmes, is seen as 'the first truly modern, scientific detective' (Binyon, 16). Medical detectives developed as a sub-category (see Binyon, 1990, 25–8), while the doctor-scientist has served 'as the object of considerable cultural anxiety, from Mary Shelley's Dr. Frankenstein to Hollywood's mad scientist' (Raylene Ramsay in Merivale and Sweeney, 1999, 204).

Todorov (1977, 51–2) has pointed out that suspense tended to replace mystery in detective fiction, as the thriller succeeded the whodunit. Poe had long ago promulgated his 'metaliterary tales' (Todorov, 1991, 102) – a phenomenon carried on in the twentieth century, from Borges to Robbe-Grillet. Merivale and Sweeney (1999, 19) also draw attention to 'the merging of two popular genres, the detective story and the historical novel', for example in works by Eco and Peter Ackroyd – not (as we have already seen) that this is of itself exactly new. According to one contemporary cultural commentator, Mark Lawson, the disaster movie, in effect, replaced the Gothic novel of old, to exorcise communal fears – and this itself is now being overtaken by television and cinematic drama-documentary.[30]

Many of these trends and features combined or conspired to form what has become known as 'metaphysical detection' (see Merivale and Sweeney, 1999, and in particular their introductory essay, 'The Game's Afoot: On the Trail of the Metaphysical Detective Story': 1–24). This latter phrase is said to have been coined by Howard Haycraft, writing in 1941, referring back to 'the paradoxical plots and philosophico-theological intentions' of G.K. Chesterton (in the Father Brown tales).[31] The Christian (more specifically Catholic) drenching (to reiterate Knight's designation) supplied by Chesterton was subsequently 'secularized by Borges and other proto-postmodernist writers of experimental fiction like Felipe Alfau, Vladimir Nabokov and Flann O'Brien' (Merivale and Sweeney, 1999, 4). Metaphysical detection is a departure from, rather than a development of, psychic detection in its often ludic epistemological-ontological concerns – following one might say more the 'metaliterary tale', through Romanticism, modernism and high modernism into postmodernist textual practices.

However, elements of the occult or psychic traditions may still remain amid the metaliterary patchwork, or here and there resurface. Eco's *Foucault's Pendulum* (already referred to above as an occult extravaganza) may be a postmodern semiotic thriller and a diabolical blockbuster – but in the arcane Hermetic and cabalistic learned tradition. Far removed from sensational drivel in the manner of certain recent works, it nevertheless gave rise (as did indeed *The Da Vinci Code*) to protests from the Vatican. In this work, built on an erudite *bricolage* of historical, philosophical, pseudo-scientific and religio-apocryphal-heretical texts, a trio of esoteric sleuths discern (or rather invent) a vast centuries-wide 'Plan' encompassing and controlling human history, from the Druids to the present day, designed to control the world by mastery of its telluric currents. 'It is as if', one commentator puts it, 'the detectives in this novel are governed by the principle that the wilder the interpretation, the more valid the description of events' (Joel Black in Merivale and Sweeney, 1999, 88).

Another literary theorist turned novelist is Julia Kristeva: 'I am writing this metaphysical – or is it psychological? – crime novel' (Kristeva, 2006, 62), notes the narrator of *Murder in Byzantium* (*Meurtre à Byzance*, 2004). It is, of course, both – as well as (once again) the rewriting of history as imaginative fiction in a modern technological vein. Against a complex procedure of psychological and historical unravelling, a killer is murdering members of a dubious religious cult, while a missing prominent historian of the Crusades has strangled his pregnant research assistant. The detection team here are not exactly of the psychic persuasion, but such questions are asked as: 'But what is a ghost?' 'A being condemned to impalpability by death, absence, or a change of habits' (ibid., 204) – is one of the answers supplied.

'Remote telepathy' makes a recent reappearance in *The Oxford Murders* by Guillermo Martínez (2005), allegedly modelled on a story 'in an old edition of *Ellery Queen's Mystery Magazine*' (see Martínez, 164–6) along with 'remote hypnosis' (192) – although Huysmans' *The Damned*, it should be pointed out (back in 1891), had discussed murder by telepathy and hypnosis. In David Mitchell's story *Acknowledgements* (2005), the narrator is something of a psychic murderer, as opposed to a psychic detective. The instigator and chronicler of the phenomenon of 'Psychomigration', he finds himself impelled to return to his old school (though not exactly in the style of Blackwood's 'Secret Worship') to avenge himself on his old caning headmaster – now helplessly communing with him from a hospice.[32]

*   *   *   *   *

One curiosity ever likely to recur in crime fiction, one may apparently rest assured, remains the type of mental leap, or inspired guess, that can take the form of, or appear tantamount to, the psychic hunch. Something 'not much more than a *guess*' may be all there is – in a situation such as that highlighted in Matthew Pearl's second novel, *The Poe Shadow* (2006): 'inferior to trained practices of reasoning' as such a concept may be, nevertheless, 'to guess is one of the most elevated and indestructible powers of the human mind, a far more interesting art than reasoning or demonstration because it comes to us directly from imagination' (Pearl, 2006, 346). Moreover, according to one of the so-called 'secret chapters' of *The Poe Shadow*: 'The ratiocinator appears to those uninitiated observers to possess powers that are nearly divine – or demonic'.[33]

Pearl's first novel, *The Dante Club* (2003), invokes, both in theme and detail, 'a murky antechamber into an other-world' (Pearl, 2003, 28), along with 'Lucifer' and the respective hells of Milton and Dante (ibid., 212), amid a fair sprinkling of apocalyptic imagery. A team of translators and enthusiasts, headed by the poet Longfellow and Oliver Wendell Holmes (medical professor and poet), are pushing the first American version of *The Divine Comedy* through a reluctant Harvard in 1865 (the six hundredth anniversary of Dante's birth), when a spate of *Inferno*-esque murders breaks out.[34] In consequence, 'the Dante Club was working primarily with what they could find literarily and the police with what they could find physically' (145). A division within the Club is created between 'a company of investigators [or literary detectives] and a company of translators' (234). 'Dante's Hell is part of our world as much as part of the underworld', affirms James Russell Lowell, another of the group (43). And so indeed it proves. Just as Dante's *Divina Commedia* was divided into three 'canticles', so is Pearl's novel. Investigation is subdivided into three denominations: the Dante Club, the 'good' police of Boston and the malevolent rival detective force (not counting the interferences of an employee of the Pinkerton agency). A further triad of sectarian rivalries – Calvinism, Unitarianism and Catholicism – subsides by the novel's end from a threatened downpour into 'a gentle, Christian rain' (367).

Pearl's second work of investigative researched fiction deals with the mysteries surrounding the death of Edgar Poe in the Baltimore of 1849.[35] Mostly a first-person narrative on the part of Quentin Clark (lawyer and would-have-been legal defender of Poe), *The Poe Shadow* also incorporates Parisian scenes (from 1851), to reinhabit key Poe stories (at the same time not unreminiscent of the historical French settings noted above in works by Hoffmann, Collins and Le Fanu). Poe's concept of 'ratiocination' achieves stress and definitions pushing it perhaps further in the direction of metaphysical detection (see Pearl, 2006, 11, 106, 111); beyond 'mere "calculus" or "logic"', it is poised 'to achieve analysis' through 'the heights of imagination'. Minor characters can be 'the Phantom' or a 'printer's devil' – not to mention the invocation of 'resurrection men' – while one significant figure can effect disguises of 'demonic transformation' (ibid., 184), verging on actual shape-shifting, or William Wilson-like doubling (see 180). Again, we have a trio of investigators: two supposed Dupin models (an Auguste Duponte and a Baron Claude Dupin), along with the growing detective role of Clark himself. And there is a further triad of less efficient investigative bodies, comprising the Sons of Temperance, the Baltimore police and meddlesome French agents.

A further work of investigative research featuring historical figures is Jed Rubenfeld's *The Interpretation of Murder* (2006), a novel which embroiders fictionally upon the actual visit to New York, in 1909, of Freud and Jung. This scenario permits the introduction of, if not a psychic then a psychoanalytical form of detection, along with traditional deduction, carried out by an American disciple of Freud (though not without some theoretical questioning) and a smart up-and-coming New York police officer. Freud himself maintains a usefully benevolent (and Jung a somewhat less benevolent) background presence.

If Pearl's *The Poe Shadow* returns us, in a sense at least, to positions and locations close to our starting points, another recent launch-pad into this now familiar subgenre of fiction-alised investigative research takes us on, or back again, to our high point of psychic detection, the Edwardian era. Julian Barnes's novel *Arthur & George* (2005) deals largely with the intervention of Arthur Conan Doyle in the case of the wrongly convicted Staffordshire lawyer, George Edalji – a victim of racial and personal prejudice, combined with malevolently fanciful 'detection'. Under the most improbable circumstances, involving purportedly self-inflicted poison-pen campaigns and a 'case of the locked room in reverse' (Barnes, 2005, 209), Edalji becomes the scapegoat to 'pure speculation' (ibid., 279) on the part of the Staffordshire police, from chief constable down – speculative guessing that might as well have been supposed 'psychic' in origin (as is in effect suggested: 255).

Doyle's own methods of deduction and investigation in the Edalji case (which indeed helped bring into being the Court of Appeal) bear a considerable resemblance to those of Sherlock Holmes (with Doyle's amanuensis, 'Woodie', acting as something of the Watson figure). We have already noted the Holmesian reaction to anything calling for, or smacking of, psychic detection. However, this was not an attitude shared by Doyle himself, who had long frequented seances, though being more impressed by telepathy than Mesmerism (39–40).[36] At the request of the Society for Psychical Research (which he had joined some years earlier: see 64), Doyle assisted in the investigation of a haunted house in Dorset in 1906, in a set of circumstances similar to a number of the haunted house stories outlined above (see

222–3). Later he tried psychic methods over the disappearance of Agatha Christie (331–2).

Having invented and developed the arch-rationalist Holmes, then, Doyle was nevertheless himself, in his time, medical practitioner, psychic detective, psychic (indeed burgeoning Spiritualist) and finally – according to some at least – 'spirit'. Thus Doyle might even be seen as following in the (spiritual) footsteps of certain of our Starmen (from Chapter 2). The memorial meeting following his death, held at the Albert Hall (on 13 July 1930) under the auspices of the Marylebone Sipritualist Association (and chaired by a Mr George Craze), to include, at the request of the second Lady Doyle, 'a demonstration of clairvoyance' (327), attracted up to ten thousand participants (plus, allegedly, an unknown number of spirits). Doyle's last 'authenticated' manifestation occurred at a seance in 1937. Since then, from the otherworld, or some other plane, he may even now keep watch over the rise, fall, and possibly the rise again, of at least the fictional psychic detective.

Notes

1 T.J. Binyon (1990, 10–11) points out the popularisation and 'perpetuated misuse of the term "deduction", a misuse which is now so common as not to be worth avoiding. Strictly speaking, a deduction is an instance drawn out from a generality. If all Cretans are liars and the man before us is a Cretan, we deduce that he is a liar'. This is very different from the types of 'mental leap' made by Sherlock Holmes – more properly designated 'inferences', partaking of 'the nature of all circumstantial evidence: though the degree of probability increases as each successive inference supports its predecessors, certainty can never be obtained'.

2 Émile Gaboriau (1832–73): see Knight, 2004, 48–51. Gaboriau's protagonist, Monsieur Lecoq, rather like Sherlock Holmes in detective fiction in English, has been held up as a model, and indeed still is: he is seen as an inspiration for Victor Legris in the (historically set) novels of Claude Izner, such as *La disparue du*

Père-Lachaise (2003), trans. Lorenza Garcia and Isabel Reid as *The Père-Lachaise Mystery* (London: Gallic Books, 2007).

3 Thomas De Quincey, 'On Murder Considered as One of the Fine Arts', *Blackwood's Edinburgh Magazine*, 21, 122 (Feb. 1827), pp. 140–63 (see Worthington, 2005, 21–8 on De Quincey's contributions).

4 The converse of the 'private eye' (a hired sleuth, investigating ['eye' being 'i', short for 'investigator': *Encarta WED*] discreetly and reporting solely to an employer) is seemingly intended in Alasdair Gray's use of 'the public eye' (ubiquitous investigative – or purely curious – surveillance, communicated to a worldwide audience): see his futuristic satire *A History Maker* (Edinburgh: Canongate, 1994). One is also reminded of Nabokov's novella *The Eye* (*Sogliadatai*, 1930; English version 1965), noted by Susan Elizabeth Sweeney (Merivale and Sweeney, 1999, 256–8). For a systematic differentiation between the categories of 'private detective' and 'private eye', see Binyon (1990, 32).

5 Schiller's *The Ghost-seer* may have been part of an Enlightenment onwards debunking of aspects of such texts as *Le Comte de Gabalis* by the Abbé Monfaucon de Villars (originally dating from 1670), which, along with the writings of Paracelsus and others, had a considerable Romantic impact (not least on such authors as Hoffmann and Odoevsky, on to Huysmans) and perhaps influenced early depictions of detection.

6 For a further survey of the range and nature of ghosts in literature, see also Cornwell (1999).

7 The highlight of the latter tale is surely its epigraph: 'There are but two classes of persons in the world – those who are hanged, and those who are not hanged; and it has been my lot to belong to the former' (Morrison and Baldick, 1995, 73).

8 Varley happened to produce *A Treatise on Zodiac Physiognomy* in 1828 (I am grateful to Terry Hale for this information).

9 On this collection, see George Locke, *Spectrum of Fantasy: The Bibliography and Biography of a Collection of Fantastic Literature*, London: Ferret, 1980 (III, 156a). Again, I am grateful to Terry Hale for this information.

10 Other post-Todorov commentators have refined or expanded his terms, examples and explanations somewhat, but Todorov's basic ideas retain considerable currency. See the survey

of this branch of narrative theory in Part One of Cornwell (1990).

11 On the career of Saint-Germain, literary and otherwise, see Neil Cornwell, '"You've heard of the Count Saint-Germain: . . ." – in Pushkin's "The Queen of Spades" and Far Beyond', *New Zealand Slavonic Journal. Festschrift in honour of Arnold McMillin*, 36, 2002, pp. 49–66.

12 Samuel Warren, *Passages from the Diary of a Late Physician* (1830–7; collected 1838; 1842); *The Experiences of a Barrister, and Confessions of an Attorney*, attributed to Samuel Warren (1859), may have been written by Sir James Stephen. On these see Worthington, 2005, ch. 2. Three examples of the former are included in Morrison and Baldick, 1995.

13 Luckhurst (2002, 1) defines telepathy as: 'forms of occult relation or communication between people at a distance' – 'an ancient belief, common to many cultures'.

14 Faber is 'a clear model for Van Helsing' in Stoker's *Dracula* (Luckhurst, 2002, 212n.).

15 Any knowledge of that particular Odoevsky work in western Europe is extremely improbable, given that (unlike several other of his stories) no translation of *The Salamander* appears to have been made until that by Johannes van Guenther in the volume *Magische Novellen* (Munich, 1924). The explanation for such similarities must lie in common interests and sources. Roberts, 1990, 158, 161, mentions Bulwer-Lytton's interest in Saint-Martin, Paracelsus and Cornelius Agrippa, among others – all of whom were figures of great interest to Odoevsky (cf. 'Odoyevsky and the Philosophical Tradition', in Cornwell, 1986, 91–114).

16 Dickens's story 'The Signal-Man' (1866) includes a similar element of psychic intuition, but is devoid of both detection and criminality.

17 Van Helsing's theory derived overtly (Stoker, 1996, 342) from the nineteenth-century moral and criminological theories respectively of Max Nordau and Cesare Lambroso (ibid., 389). See also Haining and Tremayne, 1997, 131–3, on Professor Arminius Vambéry.

18 For fuller readings of *Dracula*, see Cornwell, 1990, 106–12 (and the critical references therein); Showalter, 1992, 179–84, for gender-relations; Gelder, 1994, 65–85; Rickels, 1999;

Hughes, 2003, who supplies a 'post-colonial' analysis; and, on 'trance', Luckhurst, 2002, 210–13. For background to *Dracula*, see Haining and Tremayne, 1997. For literary predecessors, see Frayling, 1992; Gelder, 1994; Rickels, 1999.

19 *The Complete John Silence Stories* (1997) comprise the five novella-length works published in *John Silence – Physician Extraordinary* (1908), plus a sixth Silence story, 'A Victim of Higher Space', which, 'although written at about the same time' (Joshi, intro. to Blackwood, 1997, vii), was not published until 1917.

20 According to William Hughes (2005), 'the explanation is given in terms which apply an accredited theory – the oscillating or wave theories of light and sound – to spectra which are, rather like infra-red or ultra-violet radiation, beyond conventional perception'.

21 On Hodgson's Carnacki stories, see Briggs, 1977, 63–5; Gerald Suster's brief introduction to Hodgson (1980); and Cornwell, 1990, 146–7. For present purposes, we shall treat all nine Carnacki stories as authentic, although there are suggestions that three stories added in the 'expanded' version issued in 1947 (Sauk City, WI: Mycroft and Moran), almost three decades after Hodgson's death, might have more to do with its compiler, the Lovecraft and Hodgson enthusiast, August W. Derleth.

22 'The Haunted *Jarvee*' (Hodgson, 1980, 163–82). Hodgson (1877–1918) had been a sailor and his other books include two with sea settings: *The Boats of the Glen Carrig* (1907) and *The Ghost Pirates* (1909).

23 Aleister Crowley, *The Scrutinies of Simon Iff*, Chicago: Teitan Press, 1987, contains six of these stories. For fuller listed details, see www.redflame93.com/DeskS.html

24 Sax Rohmer, *The Dream Detective: Being Some Account of the Methods of Moris Klaw*, London: Jerrolds, 1920.

25 Twelve stories were collected under the title of *The Mysterious Mr. Quin*, London: Collins, 1930.

26 Writing on other works by Hodgson, in particular the dark fantasy novel *The Night Land* (1912), Kelly Hurley entitles her essay 'The Modernist Abominations of William Hope Hodgson': see *Gothic Modernisms*, ed. Andrew Smith and

Jeff Wallace, Basingstoke and New York: Palgrave, 2001, 129–49.

27 Dostoevsky's name is mentioned in the text (Whitehead, 2005, 240), although Rayfield (1999, 23) affirms that only a few years later did Chekhov admit to acquiring and reading Dostoevsky's works.

28 On this work, see Rayfield, 1999, 127–9 (plus the critical references listed by him: 273–4). Boris Akunin's novel *Pelagia & The Black Monk* certainly employs detection, but not in a psychic form (notwithstanding the conventual status of its eponymous investigator).

29 For much, if not everything, surrounding these series of psychic detection, see *Reading the Vampire Slayer: An Unofficial Critical Companion to Buffy and Angel*, ed. Roz Kaveney, London: Tauris Parke, 2001.

30 Mark Lawson, 'Reality is catastrophic', *Guardian*, 26 May 2006, p. 36.

31 G.K. Chesterton, *The Innocence of Father Brown* (1911) and subsequent collections, plus his *The Man Who Was Thursday* (1908): see Merivale and Sweeney (1999, *passim*); Binyon, on 'Priests, Missionaries and Rabbis' (1990, 64–6); and Knight, 2004, 75–6.

32 David Mitchell, 'Acknowledgements', *Prospect*, Oct. 2005, 60–6.

33 'Series 2: The Humboldt Incident' (Part II of III). These 'secret chapters' can be reached via the Matthew Pearl website: www. matthewpearl.com/poe/chapters.html

34 Huysmans, in *The Damned* (2001, 58), naming 'a man called Longfellow' as 'High Priest of the New Evocative Magism', apparently 'confuses the American poet with a Scots occultist and Satanist of the same name' (ibid., 270, n. 6).

35 The narrator (and presumably Pearl himself) prefer the appellation 'Edgar Poe' to 'Edgar Allan Poe', on the grounds that 'John Allan had taken in the poet as a young child in 1810, but later ungenerously abandoned him to the whims of the world' (Pearl, 2006, 29).

36 Doyle did, however, compose two early (non-Holmesian) 'mesmeric' tales: 'John Barrington Cowles: The Story of a Medical Student' (1888) and 'The Parasite: A Mesmeric and Hypnotic Mystery' (1894). On these, see Luckhurst, 2002, 205–7.

References and further reading

Primary sources

Barnes, Julian, 2005, *Arthur & George*, London: Jonathan Cape.

Blackwood, Algernon, 1997, *The Complete John Silence Stories*, ed. S.T. Joshi, Mineola, NY: Dover Publications.

Bulwer-Lytton, Edward, 2000, *The Haunted and the Haunters and Other Gothic Tales*, ed. William Lawrence, Knebworth, Herts: Able Publishing; *The Haunted and the Haunters; or The House and the Brain*, pp. 135–59.

Bulwer-Lytton, Edward, [no date] *A Strange Story, Complete*, eBook # EO6477, O'Brien's Book Cellar.

Collins, Wilkie, [no date] *After Dark*, Doylestown, PENN: Wildside Press; *The Lawyer's Story of A Stolen Letter*, pp. 47–62 (also in Cassiday, 1983, 144–60, as *The Stolen Letter*); *The French Governess's Story of Sister Rose*, pp. 71–159; *The Nun's Story of Gabriel's Marriage*, pp. 195–232; *The Professor's Story of The Yellow Mask*, pp. 241–328.

Dickens, Charles, [no date] *Christmas Books, Tales and Sketches*, Garden City, NY: Nelson Doubleday; *The Trial for Murder*, pp. 734–43.

Doyle, Sir Arthur Conan, [1928] 1953, *Sherlock Holmes: The Complete Short Stories*, London: John Murray.

Hodgson, William Hope, 1980, *Carnacki the Ghost-Finder*, London: Sphere Books.

Hoffmann, E.T.A., 2002, *Mademoiselle de Scudéri: A Tale of the Times of Louis XIV*, trans. Andrew Brown, London: Hesperus Press (also in Cassiday, 1983, 30–66, adapted, as *Mademoiselle de Scudéry*).

Huysmans, J.-K., 2001, *The Damned (Là-Bas)*, trans. Terry Hale, Harmondsworth: Penguin.

Kristeva, Julia, 2006, *Murder in Byzantium*, trans. C. Jon Delogu, New York: Columbia University Press.

Le Fanu, J. Sheridan, 1990, *In a Glass Darkly*, Gloucester: Alan Sutton.

Martínez, Guillermo, 2005, *The Oxford Murders*, trans. Sonia Soto. London: Abacus.

Odoevsky, Vladimir, 1992, *The Salamander and Other Gothic Tales*, trans. Neil Cornwell, London: Bristol Classical Press.

Odoevsky, Vladimir, 1994, *The Ghost*, in *Russian Tales of the Fantastic*, trans. Marilyn Minto, London: Bristol Classical Press, pp. 32–44.

Odoevsky, Vladimir, 1997, *Russian Nights*, trans. Olga Koshansky-Olienikov and Ralph E. Matlaw, Evanston, IL: Northwestern University Press (first pub. New York: Dutton, 1965).

Pearl, Matthew, [2003] 2004, *The Dante Club*, London: Vintage.

Pearl, Matthew, 2006, *The Poe Shadow*, London: Harvill Secker.

Poe, Edgar Allan, 1966, *Complete Stories and Poems of Edgar Allan Poe*, Garden City, NY: Doubleday; *The Murders in the Rue Morgue*, pp. 2–26; *The Mystery of Marie Rogêt*, pp. 27–63; *The Purloined Letter*, pp. 125–38 (also in Cassiday, 1983, pp. 95–112).

Rubenfeld, Jed, [2006] 2007, *The Interpretation of Murder*, London: Headline Review.

Schiller, Friedrich von, 2003, *The Ghost-seer* (*Geisterseher*, 1798), trans. Andrew Brown, London: Hesperus Press.

Stoker, Bram, 1996, *Dracula*, intro. and notes by Maud Ellmann, Oxford: Oxford University Press.

Anthologies

Cassiday, Bruce, ed., 1983, *Roots of Detection: The Art of Deduction before Sherlock Holmes*, New York: Frederick Ungar.

Luckhurst, Roger, ed., 2005, *Late Victorian Gothic Tales*, Oxford: Oxford University Press.

Morrison, Robert and Chris Baldick, eds, 1995, *Tales of Terror from Blackwood's Magazine*, Oxford: Oxford University Press.

Secondary sources

Binyon, T.J., 1990, *'Murder Will Out': The Detective in Fiction*, Oxford: Oxford University Press.

Briggs, Julia, 1977, *Night Visitors: The Rise and Fall of the English Ghost Story*, London: Faber.

Cornwell, Neil, 1986, *The Life, Times and Milieu of V.F. Odoyevsky, 1804–1869*, London: The Athlone Press.

Cornwell, Neil, 1990, *The Literary Fantastic: From Gothic to Postmodernism*, New York and London: Harvester Wheatsheaf.

Cornwell, Neil, 1998, *Vladimir Odoevsky and Romantic Poetics*, Providence and Oxford: Berghahn Books.

Cornwell, Neil, 1999, 'Ghost Writers in the Sky (and Elsewhere): Notes Towards a Spectropoetics of Ghosts and Ghostliness', *Gothic Studies*, 1, 2, pp. 156–68.

Cornwell, Neil, 2003, 'Pushkin and Odoevsky: the "Afro-Finnish" Theme in Russian Gothic', in *Empire and the Gothic: The Politics of Genre*, ed. Andrew Smith and William Hughes, Basingstoke and New York: Palgrave Macmillan, pp. 69–87.

Frayling, Christopher, 1992, *Vampyres: Lord Byron to Count Dracula*, London: Faber.

Gelder, Ken, 1994, *Reading the Vampire*, London: Routledge.

Haining, Peter and Peter Tremayne, 1997, *The Un-Dead: The Legend of Bram Stoker and Dracula*, London: Constable.

Hughes, William, 2003, 'A Singular Invasion: Revisiting the Postcoloniality of Bram Stoker's *Dracula*', in *Empire and the Gothic: The Politics of Genre*, ed. Andrew Smith and William Hughes, Basingstoke and New York: Palgrave Macmillan, pp. 99–102.

Hughes, William, 2005, ' "This strange personality that has been haunting you": Redefining Ghosts and Psychic Doctors in Algernon Blackwood's *John Silence*', unpub. paper.

Knight, Stephen, 2004, *Crime Fiction, 1800–2000: Detection, Death, Diversity*, Basingstoke and New York: Palgrave Macmillan.

Luckhurst, Roger, 2002, *The Invention of Telepathy*, Oxford: Oxford University Press.

Merivale, Patricia and Susan Elizabeth Sweeney, eds, 1999, *Detecting Texts: The Metaphysical Detective Story from Poe to Postmodernism*, Philadelphia: University of Pennsylvania Press.

Ramsey, Cynthia C., 1999, 'Gothic Treatment of the Crisis of Engendering in Odoevskii's *The Salamander*', in *The Gothic-Fantastic in Nineteenth-Century Russian Liiterature*, ed. Neil Cornwell, Amsterdam and Atlanta, GA: Rodopi, pp. 145–69.

Rayfield, Donald, 1999, *Understanding Chekhov: A Critical Study of Chekhov's Prose and Drama*, London: Bristol Classical Press.

Rickels, Laurence A., 1999, *The Vampire Lectures*, Minneapolis and London: University of Minnesota Press.

Roberts, Marie, 1990, *Gothic Immortals: The Fiction of the Brotherhood of the Rosy Cross*, London: Routledge.

Royle, Nicholas, 2003, *The uncanny*, Manchester: Manchester University Press.

Showalter, Elaine, 1992, *Sexual Anarchy: Gender and Culture at the Fin de Siècle*, London: Virago.

Sucur, Slobodan, 2001, *Poe, Odoyevsky, and Purloined Letters*, Frankfurt: Peter Lang.

Todorov, Tzvetan, 1973, *The Fantastic: A Structural Approach to a Literary Genre*, trans. Richard Howard, Cleveland and London: Case Western Reserve (first pub. as *Introduction à la littérature fantastique*, Paris, 1970).

Todorov, Tzvetan, 1977, *The Poetics of Prose*, trans. Richard Howard, Oxford: Basil Blackwell (first pub. as *La Poétique de la prose*, Paris, 1971).

Todorov, Tzvetan, 1991, *Genres in Discourse*, trans. Catherine Porter, Cambridge: Cambridge University Press (first pub. as *Genres du discours*, Paris, 1978).

Whitehead, Claire, 2005, 'Playing at Detectives: Parody in *The Swedish Match*', in *Chekhov 2004: Chekhov special issues in two volumes. Vol. 1, Aspects of Chekhov*. Essays in Poetics publications, No. 10, ed. Joe Andrew and Robert Reid, Keele: EIP, pp. 229–46.

Worthington, Heather, 2005, *The Rise of the Detective in Early Nineteenth-Century Popular Fiction*, Basingstoke and New York: Palgrave Macmillan.

4

Monk: duelling confession within the novel

<blockquote>What is there to tell [. . .]? We have no personal story. The life of any one monk is the same as any other . . .

(Ervin [Father Severinus]: Antal Szerb, *Journey by Moonlight*, p. 111)</blockquote>

This fourth and final chapter will attempt to see where the Father Zosima biographical duelling episode of *The Karamazov Brothers* can take us, when considered along with certain predecessors (episodes from works by Odoevsky and Manzoni), and indeed then some of its successors, with regard to the appearance in fiction of duels, monks and confession. Zosima is, no doubt, as has been remarked, 'a composite literary image' (Grigorieff, 1967, 34). Sergei Hackel (1983, 162–4) has proposed Bishop Bienvenu, from Hugo's *Les Misérables*, as one ingredient.

Dostoevsky's last novel, *The Karamazov Brothers* (*Brat'ia Karamazovy*, 1879–80), not counting of course the intended succeeding volumes never written, spans getting on for a thousand pages, comprising four parts, in twelve books and an epilogue.[1] While 'confession' plays a considerable part overall in the unfolding of this novel, particularly striking is the embedded story, or purported autobiography, of the *Starets* (or Elder) Zosima, which comes in Part Two, Book Six ('A Russian Monk'): 'From the life of the Schemahieromonk Father Zosima, resting in the Lord, in his own words, as recorded by Aleksei Fyodorovich Karamazov', to give the chapter its full heading (*KB*, 358–91; *PSS*, 14, 260–83).[2] It has been emphasised (by Robin F. Miller, 1990, 105) that 'Dostoevsky wrote of this section containing Zosima's narrative, "The whole novel is written for its sake . . ."'. Central, in whatever sense, to the work as a whole, Zosima's story, considered as saint's life (*zhitie*), incomplete *vita* or confession (although, in 'an unusual manoeuvre for a hagiographer', presented in the first person: Thompson, 1991, 97), comes almost at the novel's halfway point.

Although supposedly Zosima's dying-day confession, it is admitted by the narrator-chronicler that Aleksei's account (presented in Zosima's 'own words') also includes material related by the Elder-*Starets* on previous occasions, combined here to form his (written) 'autobiography'.[3] Aleksei (or Alyosha) is therefore the 'author' of a literary work, written down some considerable time after the event ('based entirely on his memories which the narrator inserts *in toto*') – points stressed by Diane Thompson (1991, 31 and, in more detail, 94–106; Leatherbarrow, 1992, 75). The biographical part of Zosima's 'manuscript', it has also been stressed by W.J. Leatherbarrow (1992, 76–9) condenses within itself 'variations on the novel's main themes'.

Zosima has been drawn to Alyosha largely because he reminds him so much, physically and 'spiritually', of the elder brother he once had: 'At the dawn of my days, when I was still a child, I had an elder brother who died in his youth, before my very eyes, only seventeen years of age', without whose existence 'I don't think I would ever have become a monk and entered upon this precious path' (356 / 259). The story of the demise from consumption of Zosima's elder brother, Markel, and his spiritual leave-taking and apparent conversion, when Zosima (then called Zinovy) is aged nine (358–62 / 260–3) leads, after a scriptural intermission, on to 'Zosima's youth' and 'the duel' (369–77 / 268–73).

Zinovy is then enrolled in the cadet corps in St Petersburg by his mother ('although not without a good many tears':

362 / 263). After his mother's death three years later (from 'grieving and worrying about us both': 363 / 263) and eight years in the cadet corps, Zinovy enters adulthood as an officer, and is posted to a provincial town. Here, misunderstandings in a supposed courtship cause a grudge, leading to a challenge, responded to through jealousy, and a duel. On the night before the duel, Zinovy strikes his batman savagely in the face; conscience-stricken over this, he remembers the example of his brother Markel, and the next morning makes fawning amends to his servant. Fired upon from twelve paces and lightly grazed, Zinovy then aborts his shot, hurling his pistol into the trees, and apologises to his opponent for the offence he had caused him. This leads to immediate protests, from his adversary and from his second: 'It's a disgrace to the regiment to ask for pardon right at the firing line' (374 / 271). Zinovy (soon to be Zosima) has manipulated the protocols of duelling to his own (newly found) spiritual ends, although, it has to be recognised, 'he didn't flinch from being shot at' (375 / 272). Upon announcing his intention to resign his commission and enter a monastery, Zinovy even becomes a popular social figure ('a monk can't be sentenced': ibid.), although to some (the authorities seemingly included) he remains something of a figure of fun.

This situation evolves somewhat, prior to Zinovy's departure into the monastic world to become Zosima, and eventually an Elder, due to an episode involving a mysterious middle-aged resident of the town, eventually named just as Mikhail ('The mysterious visitor': 377–91 / 273–83). This mystery man, inspired by Zinovy's conduct over the duel, comes to him with a confession of his own: of a murder he had committed years before, escaping justice by cunning. Mikhail, now a respected citizen and family man, determines to confess his past crime in public. This he proceeds to do (having even overcome a sudden urge to kill his interim confessor, the virtuous Zinovy), but is not believed. Sudden illness, deemed to be from mental derangement, descends on

Mikhail, who dies shortly thereafter. Some people begin to believe there might have been some truth in this confession, but in general the town turns on Zinovy, holding him to be in some way morally responsible for Mikhail's end. However, Zosima concludes, 'I maintained my silence and soon left the town for good, and five months later the Good Lord set me on a firm and righteous path' (391 / 283).

It has, it should perhaps be mentioned for future reference, been pointed out (by Sergei Hackel, 1983, 149–50), that 'even though Zosima's role as confessor is mentioned . . ., the reader is not shown him practising as such' (although he is seen in what might be something more of a counselling role). Irina Terekhova (2007, 67) also notes that there is 'not one scene of traditional church confession' in the novel. Zosima indeed features rather more as a prophet (see Thompson, 1991, 248–50).

*   *   *   *   *

We go back now to an earlier part of the century, to Alessandro Manzoni's large-scale historical novel *The Betrothed* (hereafter *B*) (*I Promessi Sposi*, first published 1827; revised for republication, in its definitive Tuscan version, 1840; hereafter *IPS*). Not far into this epic work, we encounter the figure of Father Cristoforo, a Capuchin monk, who intercedes on behalf of the ill-used eponymous couple and is exiled to Rimini for his pains. He later returns to work heroically amid the plague victims (of the 1628 Milan pestilence), himself eventually perishing from the disease.

The story of Cristoforo is told in a third-person account typical of the narrative method of *The Betrothed*, purportedly taken from 'my anonymous author' (*B* 77 / *IPS* 71), which makes up chapter 4 of the novel (*B* 76–91 / *IPS* 69–87). Originally named Lodovico (or Ludovico), this Father Cristoforo had been born the son of a rich merchant. With his education and wealth he 'had acquired the habits of a nobleman' (79 / 72); however, the fact that he was not of the nobility led to social problems. His good-natured instincts had already suggested to him 'the possibility of going into a monastery'; this idea might have remained pure fancy, had it not been 'suddenly converted into a resolution by an incident more serious than anything which had happened to him before' (80 / 74).

Lodovico, accompanied by the family household steward named Cristoforo, with a pair of bravos at heel (as was the fashion, according to the then street etiquette of the gentry), encountered a similar formation, from the opposite direction, headed by a brash nobleman. The opposing faction refused to give way, although Ludovico's precise location, with the wall standing to his right, would have given him right of way according to the codes of the time. A bloody confrontation ensued, in which the conscientious steward, anxious to protect his superior, was run through with the nobleman's sword. 'Nearly out of his mind' at this, 'Lodovico thrust his sword into the belly of the murderer, who fell dying at almost the same instant as the unfortunate Cristoforo' (82 / 76).

The altercation having taken place close to a Capuchin monastery, as the narrative proceeds the wounded Lodovico is taken in, both to be cared for 'in the hands of a brother surgeon' (83 / 77), and for purposes of sanctuary. The result of all this is that Lodovico interprets these events, and his place of refuge, as a divine sign for a monasterial destiny, making over his possessions to Cristoforo's large surviving family. At the same time he achieves a resolution of the legal problems that his situation inevitably caused. The Capuchins would not give up a man, in those circumstances, to the mercy of authorities and enemies. Lodovico would also be seen as implicitly admitting guilt, by 'imposing a form of penitence on himself' (85 / 79), thus furnishing his dead adversary's family with at least a certain satisfaction (and even 'honour'), while earning too the praise of 'the connoisseurs of points of chivalrous etiquette' (86 / 80). Lodovico did not, however, quite stop at this. Before fulfilling the immediate requirement to leave the city, following his ordination, he obtains permission to seek in person (and publicly receive) the forgiveness of the nobleman's family – through its main representative, the dead man's brother. In addition, he had chosen a name (one, as was customary, other than his own) 'which would serve as a continual reminder of the sin he had to expiate' (86 / 81), calling himself 'Brother Cristoforo'.

Manzoni wrote a historical novel, setting it in the first half of the seventeenth century. Umberto Eco affirms that 'everything that Renzo, Lucia, or Fra Cristoforo does could be done only in Lombardy in the seventeenth century' (Eco, 1984, 75; see also 49–50). Given the detailed make-up of some of the monkish tales featured here, we could suggest that this might not be indisputably and entirely the case, at least with regard to Fra Cristoforo.

An interesting minor spin-off from Manzoni's novel is the story *Borrhomeo the Astrologer*, published anonymously in *The Dublin University Magazine* (1862) and only comparatively recently attributed to its then editor, J. Sheridan Le Fanu.[4] This work is subtitled 'A Monkish Tale', a phrase relating to its supposed authorship, and not implying a Cristoforo-type figure as such. Indeed, set in the same Milanese plague (here given as 1630), it appears to play instead on the figure of Cardinal Federigo Borromeo, who, the spelling of his name apart, is transformed into the titular astrologer (or at least 'an astrologer calling himself Borrhomeo': Le Fanu, 1985, 20) – who in the text is in fact an alchemist. Rather than a heroic saintly figure, this Borrhomeo is obsessed with finding the elixir of life, and is accused of being one of the 'anointers' (*untori*) or plague-spreaders. He had himself predicted a 'pale comet', to be followed by pestilence (ibid.). Through the smoke from an exploded retort, he is visited by 'a pale young man' like 'a holy young confessor', a representative of 'the master of all alchymists' (26) and 'slave of Satan' (32). This visitor can bestow invisibility and a most unsatisfactory form of immortality – a thousand-year continuation of conscious catalepsy, lasting through and far beyond execution, impaling and premature burial. The visiting stranger may seem a somewhat debonair anticipation of the 'shabby devil' later to call on Ivan Karamazov – a key moment in Dostoevsky's novel for 'production of the uncanny' (Miller, 1990, 95; on Ivan's devil, see Thompson, 1991, 203–5; and, on Ivan's devil's voice, Leatherbarrow, 1992, 94–6). Ivan Karamazov's devil was later, to all intents and purposes, to reappear in Thomas Mann's *Doctor Faustus* (see *DF,* 214–43; and, on the connection, Butler, 1998, 323).

*　*　*　*　*

We now turn to Vladimir Odoevsky's little-known story of 1839, *The Witness* (*Svidetel'*). In this rather brief work (of around four thousand words), one Grigorii, a traveller returning to his native Russia, enters an Orthodox church, to notice a monk stretched out in a far corner. This figure recognises the intruder, and is indeed none other than his former comrade in the hussars and boyhood friend, Rostislav, formerly 'the star of the Petersburg balls' (333).[5] The remainder of the story comprises Rostislav's account of how he arrived at his present monastic status.

Shortly after Grigorii's departure abroad, Rostislav and his considerably younger brother Viacheslav had persuaded their sick mother to allow the latter to join his brother in military service, with Rostislav sworn by 'a harrowing oath' (334) to take every care and responsibility for Viacheslav. The frivolous, but apparently harmless, Viacheslav is introduced to Petersburg life and, after a requisite period of years, is commissioned as an officer. The delicate civilian elder brother of a comrade named Vetsky is part of the social circle of these officers, while remaining something of a figure of fun. Viacheslav indulges in this teasing rather more than most, and this tendency is exacerbated by a shared interest in a certain society *belle*. The limits are overstepped, in the temporary absence of Rostislav, during what amounts to the ceremonial binge marking the occasions when newly commissioned officers 'wet their epaulettes' (336). The cautious elder Vetsky refuses to join a childish inebriated session of jumps from a high window, and is branded for his pains a 'coward' by Viacheslav (337). 'A blow with a glove across the face was the reply' (338).

Following his own careless lapse, Rostislav is in an impossible situation with regard to any prevention of a bloody outcome. Perhaps surprisingly, the 'tail-coated civil servant' proves resolute in this final defence of his reputation; despite a policy of avoiding trouble and danger, he will 'never back off, even a step', when such things are unavoidable (338–9). Social codes and precepts of the time leave him with no other answer. A drastic miscalculation by Rostislav (as his brother's second) results in a 'homicidal arrangement' over the conditions of the duel, in which it is the elder Vetsky who remains 'as cold as ice' (340). The expected accurate marksmanship of Viacheslav does not transpire. Vetsky incurs a shoulder wound from Viacheslav's premature shot, with the right (and the physical ability still) to fire back at his opponent from point-blank range. Remembering the words of their mother, Rostislav intervenes by attempting to shield his brother – losing all sense of 'honour, conscience and the rules of society' (340–1). He is promptly dragged away, amid a general cry of disapproval: 'A shot rang out – and Viacheslav dropped as though dead', which indeed he soon was (341). Any attempt at brotherly vengeance is immediately stopped by the company of fellow-officers.

'What more is there to tell you?', the recluse continues, and he concludes:

> You know about the consequences of duels. But the punishment for my misdemeanour to me was nothing: my punishment was in my heart. My life was at an end. I wished for only one thing: either to lose my unneeded life in battle with an enemy, or to bury myself alive. I was not favoured with the first honour. Here, far from my native parts, not known

> to anyone, I am trying through lamentation and sorrow to stifle the voice of my own heart. But to this day dreadful visions awaken me at night ... my mother, dying in despair ... and in my ears ring the terrible words of the scripture: '*Cain, where is thy brother?*' (341)

Permanent reclusion in this monastery has been the result.

*   *   *   *   *

Further back, towards the heyday of the English Gothic novel, dubious monks and confessions are to be found aplenty. A striking example is Ann Radcliffe's *The Italian, or the Confessional of the Black Penitents: A Romance* (to give it its full and, in this sense, revealing title), of 1797.[6] The opening prologue (Radcliffe, 1987, 1–4) depicts an English fascination with the whole phenomenon of confession, introducing a lurking 'assassin', given sanctuary in a 'Black Penitent' convent near Naples, who is, however, himself said to have 'no relation' with the lengthy story to be related. There follows the 'romance' (of Vivaldi and Ellena), which comes surrounded by a farrago of mysterious and treacherous brethren: principal among them Father Schedoni (frequently dubbed 'the Confessor'); plus a sinister monk eventually revealed as Father Nicola di Zampari; 'the grand penitentiary Ansaldo'; and various officers of the Inquisition (including a 'vicar-general'). Actual confessions are frequently alluded to, and conversations occur that are said to be 'Sacred as a confession!' (ibid., 172). Criminal conspiracies are plotted or acknowledged in such proceedings, including murder (of a brother, attempted murder of a wife and conspiracy to murder others). Disclosure of confessions may occur, if only (supposedly) by Inquisitional order; deathbed confessions can become formal depositions. Family feuds among the dysfunctional nobility can readily, it seems, drive either perpetrators or victims into the cloisters, or even into the welcoming arms of the Inquisition. 'Cloisters and prison tend to merge', for instance, later too in the work of

Huysmans, as Victor Brombert has remarked, in relation particularly to Huysmans' novel *La Cathédrale* (1898).[7] Ellen Scaruffi, in her dissertation on Odoevsky, has noted that 'The *studiolo* and the prison share a common origin in the medieval monk's cell'.[8]

One could hardly pass over the Gothic period, or this theme, without at least noticing Matthew Lewis's *The Monk* (1796). In this novel, which gave the sobriquet 'Monk' to its author, we encounter a nefarious accumulation of monastic denizens of both sexes. These can include individuals merely alluded to, such as 'a robber, who had once been a monk' who 'performed over us a burlesque rather than a religious [marriage] ceremony' (Lewis, 1959, 138), or alleged, such as a spectral bleeding nun. The young novitiate Rosario is revealed to be a woman – indeed the temptress and sorceress Matilda. Ambrosio, the supposedly saintly and immaculate 'friar' (or 'abbot') of the title, degenerates into 'the voluptuous monk', with Matilda his 'concubine' (ibid., 227), before masquerading as the confessor of the beautiful Antonia and her sick mother, and deteriorating further into murdering 'ravisher' – guilty (had he then but known it) of incest and matricide. There is also a dangerous 'domina', the murderous prioress from the convent of St. Clare; a Grand Inquisitor (and his underlings); and threats of an Auto da Fé. Diabolical appearances are later made by Lucifer – in a more traditional form than the more civilian daemonic visitors of other works here mentioned. Not surprisingly, he has little patience with 'prayers of superstitious dotards and droning monks' (413). However, at least one other character also embraces the secular, or cynical, view (presumably that being propounded by English authors, such as Lewis and Radcliffe).[9] Thus Lorenzo, at least, remains cognisant:

> Conscious that among those who chaunted the praises of their God so sweetly there were some who cloaked with devotion the foulest sins, their hymns inspired him with

> detestation at their hypocrisy. . . . His good sense had pointed out to him the artifices of the monks, and the gross absurdity of their miracles, wonders and suppositious reliques. He blushed to see his countrymen the dupes of deceptions so ridiculous, and only wished for an opportunity to free them from their monkish fetters. (334–5)

Baldesar Castiglione's *The Book of the Courtier* (1528), which is likely to have been known to English authors through Thomas Hoby's translation, *The Courtyer* of 1561, also includes a sounding off against 'friars' (Castiglione, 1994, 224–5; 'Friers': Hoby translation, 229).

Even before these novels by Radcliffe and Lewis, the Scottish writer John Moore, in his Grand Tour travelogue, *View of Society and Manners in Italy* (1781), effected some pains to dismiss '[t]he stories which circulate in Protestant countries, concerning the scandalous debauchery of monks' and Roman Catholicism's 'artful plan of imposition' upon a duped flock. However, it has been duly observed, his own prose did not differ so markedly in this respect, with a passage on the monastic sanctuary offered to assassins (following, for instance, knife fights) being closely comparable with (perhaps even influential upon) Radcliffe's already mentioned opening passage of *The Italian*.[10]

An even grimmer view of the Catholic monastic system and practices is contained within Charles Maturin's influential (particularly in Europe – Manzoni and the Russians included) Gothic novel *Melmoth the Wanderer* (1820). This may not be entirely surprising, coming as it does from the pen of an Anglo-Irish curate of Huguenot descent. The lengthy novel, itself subtitled 'A Tale', includes within it (or indeed, for most of it, stretching overall from pages 121 to 691 in the Penguin edition edited by Alethea Hayter) the embedded 'Tale of the Spaniard'. This saga, other qualities apart, provides something of an opposing version to the stories already considered in that its main purpose is to depict the struggles for escape of a young man forced into monastic vows. Maturin's one famous novel was apparently sermon-inspired, while monastic-conventual inspiration was drawn from Diderot's *La Religieuse* (see Hayter's introduction: Maturin, 1977, 9–29).

Robin Milner-Gulland has referred to *The Karamazov Brothers* as 'a ragbag of tales and tales-within-tales'.[11] This expression is nothing, if not an even more apt description of *Melmoth the Wanderer*.[12] The Spaniard (one Alonzo de Monçada) is the main structural force and protagonist of the novel (even though 'not much more than a narrative tool': Hayter in Maturin, 1977, 23), with the role of the eponymous wanderer reduced largely to that of habitual though menacing intruder. The 'tales', often embedded to multiple levels, come thick and fast, taking the form of background, anecdote, reminiscence, confession, deathbed discourse, parchment or manuscript. A vast range of monks, shown mainly in an extremely ill light, parade before the reader, from the utterly subservient to the 'contumacious' (ibid., 78, 146), the obnoxious family 'Director', superiors and inquisitors. The most sinister figure (not counting the preternatural, though lay figure, Melmoth) is the parricide who turned monk to obtain sanctuary, while remaining both open to the highest (other than the ultimate Satanic) bidder and operating as an official of the Inquisition.

Alonzo had found himself trapped in labyrinthine monastic and then inquisitional clutches, through his mother's 'confession' of his pre-wedlock birth and his consequent demotion in favour of a younger 'legitimate' brother – the whole operation, with the eldest son of a duke taking the vows, counting as 'a glorious triumph for the ex-Jesuits' (144). Although the phrase 'monastic life' had earlier 'thrilled in [his] ears' (124), such life is soon felt to be 'the wrong side of the tapestry' (125). Notwithstanding the noble (and life-costing) interventions of his younger brother, the rest of the novel is largely the protracted chronicle of Alonzo's eventual escape. Vows had been enforced through 'fraud and terror' (189), aided by fraudulent miracle, with the constant prospect of being 'murdered *conventually*' before liberation could be achieved (208).

Confession may occur through traditional means, or under great stress, or in more unorthodox ways, at the command of secret voices, through dream and the 'horrible eloquence of sleep' (278), or by 'an extorted confession' (325). There may also be such a thing as 'that incommunicable condition' forbidden to be revealed 'except in the act of confession' (322), or indeed 'tremendous secrets' that 'can never be disclosed by the confessor but to the Pope' (323). 'If only the confessional could speak!', exclaims one character in Huysmans' *The Damned* (Huysmans, 2001, 56). Occasionally, of course, it did.

Just as *The Karamazov Brothers* should have had sequels, having listened for 'many days' to the Spaniard's narrative, 'young Melmoth signified to his guest that he was prepared to hear the sequel' (Maturin, 1977, 693) – though such a follow-up narrative is not forthcoming. Maturin's one further novel (*The Albigenses*, 1824) achieved little success.

If Matthew Lewis's novel (and its successors) has a rival, or perhaps indeed a superior, as the ultimate monk novel, then such a narrative emerges from German Romanticism, in the form of E.T.A. Hoffmann's *The Devil's Elixirs* (1816). This work has been noted as paralleling Dostoevsky's last novel in several respects ('miracles, monasticism and the operation of grace in the world': Belknap, 1990b, 100–1). In this novel, the author poses modestly as the mere editor-publisher of the posthumous papers of one Brother Medardus, the Capuchin. Having imbibed 'the devil's elixirs' (a liquid to be preserved, but never taken), Medardus renounces a career of successful (if egotistical) monastic preaching, to embark on (what the editor calls) a life of 'ludicrous perversity' (Hoffmann, 1963, 2), en route from East Prussia to Rome.

A strange pattern of sensationalism and coincidence, inspired by the powers beyond and by 'Chance', accommodated to his own sinful urges, leads to a succession of actual, or apparent, crimes involving murder, rape, incest and madness. Complex family relationships and heredity inter-link with subtle mental dislocations. A divided personality supplies ghostly (or actual) doubles and disembodied spirits. Confessions are frequently made, or demanded, in a real world in which 'physicians and father-confessors are rulers, masters of body and soul' (209). Following one such even-tual disclosure, Medardus is told: 'A destiny which you could not elude gave Satan power over you, and by your crimes you merely became his tool' (248). 'The jests of hell were being played on earth', or so it seemed to Medardus (246); to one continually reappearing buffoon, however, his conduct had been 'sublime pranks' (279). A major challenge to the ability of Medardus to effect convincing disguise had been the task of dealing with his 'monastic gait' (see p. 94).[13]

Eric Blackall sees in *The Devil's Elixirs* an unusual combi-nation of the thriller, the morality play and the psychologi-cal. While the elixir itself may be a diabolical potion, or merely a rather fine old Marsala, it also represents 'the lure of the uncanny and the vicarious'; Hoffmann's novel 'is a study of the surfacing of the subconscious' – and perhaps the most powerful such 'in the whole of German romanti-cism' (Blackall, 1983, 235). It is as well a study of 'Redemp-tion through pure, transcendental Love – the Romantic doctrine proclaimed . . . from Schelling to Richard Wagner' (Ronald Taylor in Hoffmann, 1963, xi). *The Devil's Elixirs* also testifies to the transcendental power of art, both Hoff-mann's first love, music, and – here in particular – painting; more significant still, perhaps, is the fact that the prove-nance of Medardus's manuscript responds directly to the notion (ordered by the Prior: ibid., 319) of writing (indeed of written confession) as penance.

*   *   *   *   *

The main features of the extracts, or stories, discussed above – in particular those emanating from Dostoevsky, Odoevsky and Manzoni (to put them for the moment in reverse chronological order) – highlight and combine confession (whether formal or informal), monks and duelling (or comparable ritualised violence). Family members and relationships of the protagonists (especially brothers and mothers), and occasionally servants, are commonly prominent as well. These three features, or themes, will now be looked at again, in slightly more general terms, and taken in reverse order.

The transmission of fighting skills, intended to assist fighting for one's country (in battle generally or in hand-to-hand engagement), but inevitably equally suited to use in personal quarrels, led to the phenomenon of the duel – defined by Sydney Anglo as 'a personal combat fought, theoretically at least, according to certain mutually agreed conventions' (Anglo, 2000, 272–3). Well established in Mediterranean lands by the late fifteenth century, such combat was initially conducted with sword, knife and dagger. 'The early history of pistol duelling awaits its historian', we are told, but this development was certainly under way in France by the mid-seventeenth century (ibid., 318, n. 5).[14] Vladimir Nabokov, who includes multiple references to duelling in his fulsome edition of Pushkin's *Eugene Onegin*, quotes Sir Jonah Barrington to the effect that, around 1777, 'the *Fire-eaters* [duelers] were in great repute in Ireland', and makes mention of 'a MS code of honor at Clonmel' (Nabokov, 1990, 2, 150). The 'favorite Continental version', however, Nabokov resumes, expatiating in some detail on Pushkin's duelling (ibid., 3, 43–51), introduced the mid-distance stretch of ground, *la barrière*, 'a term stemming from the oldest form of any pistol duel, which was fought on horseback' (3, 43–4).

The duel in Russia, in its cultural-historical and literary contexts, has been examined too by Irina Reyfman in her book *Ritualized Violence Russian Style*. Duelling codes in printed form, she affirms, appeared 'late in the duel's history, when the live dueling tradition had begun to deteriorate' (Reyfman, 1999, 290–1, n. 9) – later still in Russia, only 'at the end of the nineteenth century'. It is also said that Italy, which had much earlier been 'the main producer of treatises on dueling and the honor code . . . itself did not know serious dueling' (ibid.). According to Anglo (2000, 36), 'in Italy, where a labyrinthine code of honour was designed to stifle the formal duel, armed affrays were commonplace'. The best guide to such matters in that country is likely to be Castiglione's *The Book of the Courtier*. Indeed, Castiglione advises:

> Just as once a woman's reputation for purity has been sullied it can never be restored, so once the reputation of a gentle-man-at-arms has been stained through cowardice or some other reproachful behaviour, even if only once, it always remains defiled in the eyes of the world and covered with ignominy. (Castiglione, 1976, 57)

The courtier should not be 'too anxious for these engage-ments, save where his honour demands it'. 'However, when a man has committed himself so far that he cannot with-draw without reproach then both in the preliminaries and in the duel itself he should be very deliberate' (ibid., 62). This is of particular interest, of course, for the case of the Manzoni episode and the 'alternative' street-skirmish, but still ritu-alised form of violence, found in that occurrence. In any event, as we are informed by Julian Pitt-Rivers (1965, 24), 'The victor in any competition for honour finds his reputa-tion enhanced by the humiliation of the vanquished. This is as true on the street-corner as in the lists'. In addition to other factors and causes, the same commentator points out, 'we should regard honorific rituals as rites of passage' (ibid., 25; see also Anglo, 2000, 37, on the psychology of such action).

In Russia duelling took place from the eighteenth century until the outbreak of the First World War. The historical record is sketchy enough, due to such factors as the personal nature of the conflicts, the inevitably biased accounts left by participants or observers, and the legal ambiguities and responses of the authorities. Writers were not infrequently duellists themselves; Pushkin and Lermontov met their early deaths duelling, and there were considerable delays in reporting the cause of death in print (six weeks in Pushkin's case, and seventeen years in that of Lermonov: Reyfman, 1999, 7, 291, n. 12).[15] Bound up with a fastidious regard for 'personal space' and 'bodily integrity' (as well as standard social and sexual conflicts), duels in Russia frequently began from, or deteriorated into, fistfights, slaps in the face and other 'unofficial parts of the dueling ritual', amid what is seen as a general 'deficiency in Russians' collective *point d'honneur* mentality' (ibid., 10). In the tradition generally, it is said, 'the punctilios of the formal duel, designed to give some semblance of structure to personal violence, were more frequently violated than observed' (Anglo, 2000, 34).

The duel as a phenomenon is thus closely connected with the military mind and the officer corps (not least, vis-à-vis the conception of war), along with concepts of, or urges towards, execution and suicide. 'Once a challenge is uttered', we are told, 'dueling logic takes over' (Reyfman, 1999, 30). The most obvious serious consequences apart, the question of challenges (or non-challenges) and refusals could lead to aspersions over honour, and even suicide, on either side – not to mention the urge to duel being itself at times suicide-driven. Personal or family honour was not the only point of contention; also called into consideration was what Reyfman terms 'corporate honor' (ibid., 255–60), or the reputation of the regiment. The 'golden age of the Russian duel' (see 73–85) was in the first quarter of the nineteenth century (in particular perhaps up to the Decembrist Revolt of 1825 and involving future Decembrists themselves). 'Especially bewildering', indeed, in the view of Reyfman (78), 'is the prevalence of senseless dueling among the intellectual elite'.

The literary depiction of duelling gathered pace over the same period. Particularly significant in this regard was the fiction of Aleksandr Bestuzhev (later mainly known by his post-Decembrist pen name of Marlinsky) – himself an experienced practitioner of *breterstvo*.[16] His 'treatment of the duel', Reyfman affirms (1999, 188), 'shaped the Russian literary tradition'.[17] The best-known duels in Russian literature take place in works by Pushkin and Lermontov, but duels are also to be found within the fiction of Turgenev and Tolstoy (who had between themselves a drawn-out dispute which might have ended in a duel), and, of course, Dostoevsky (to whose work Reyfman devotes a lengthy chapter, entitled 'How Not to Fight'). Subsequent Russian writers employing the theme of the duel include Leskov, Chekhov (in both prose and drama), Kuprin and Artsybashev. The latter's novel *Sanin* (1907) provides a notable literary example of the honour-restoring suicide: 'when Sanin refuses to fight with the officer whom he has slapped in the face [the seducer of his sister], the officer kills himself' (Reyfman, 1999, 17, 4).

In Chekhov's novella *The Duel* (*Duel'*, 1891), the event itself emanates from personal animosity (indeed 'hate') arising purportedly too from what John Tulloch calls 'false responses to science and art' (Tulloch, 1980, 124).[18] More plausible incidents of insult and sexual provocation go on in parallel, almost coincidentally. Denunciation (as part of what may be regarded as 'confession' to third parties) and dispute lead to what Tulloch terms 'the duel of cruel predators' between the feckless Laevsky and the insufferable Von Koren – the final confrontation itself being made by Chekhov into 'an absurd non-event' that diverts its partakers, to rescue and convert them from 'the blind duel of natural selection' (ibid., 127, 129, 131). A bystander to these events is the young deacon ('an unworldly, childlike ecclesiastic': Rayfield, 1999, 102), who, it is suggested, may yet shove his wife into a nunnery and become a [hiero]monk (Chekhov, 1994, 159 / Chekhov, 1962, 410), to join Von Koren's zoological expedition. Largely depicted as a supercilious ditherer, the deacon initially declines to attend the duel (as 'my orders don't allow it': ibid., 201 / 463), but still finds himself drawn to the 'heathen spectacle' (208 / 471), tempted by 'the evil one' (215 / 480). His intervening and 'despairing shout', however, saves the day, while turning the event to farce; his presence nearby, lurking in the maize, is not to be disclosed, he implores, in case he 'get into hot water with the authorities' (215 / 480–1).

An actual, albeit farcical, duel between two poets (Nikolai Gumilev and Maksimilian Voloshin), occurring in 1909, achieved satirical literary mention as well, in a story by Zinaida Gippius (*Moon Ants*, of 1910), referred to as 'The Story of a Lost Boot'; no more serious loss took place.[19] Indeed, 'Silver Age' duelling in Russia has recently earned a lengthy study to itself (which includes a survey of duels which did not take place).[20]

An interesting instance of a late proposed duel, involving his father in 1911, is described in Nabokov's *Speak, Memory*. A 'Rightist newspaper' having published 'a scurrilous piece containing insinuations that my father could not let pass', Vladimir Dmitrievich (who was to be assassinated in 1922 in Berlin) called out the editor – 'since the well-known rascality of the actual author of the article made him "non-duelable" (*neduelesposobnïy*, as the Russian dueling code had it)' (Nabokov, 1969, 147). No duel in fact took place, as 'the challenge had [eventually] been met by an apology' (ibid., 150). The younger Vladimir recalls his youthful excitement and anxiety: 'No Russian writer of any repute had failed to describe *une rencontre*, a hostile meeting, always of course of the classical *duel à volonté* type (not the ludicrous back-to-back-march-face-about-bang-bang per-formance of movie and cartoon fame)' (149). The already near-anachronism of this (in the end) non-event did not escape notice in the press: 'Sly digs were taken at [Nabokov senior's] having reverted to a feudal custom that he had criticized in his own writings' (147). Brief allusion to an 'alternative' (farcical enough, but eventually fatal) version of this occurs to eliminate the father (purportedly in 1913) in the first chapter of *The Real Life of Sebastian Knight* (Nabokov, 1995, 6, 11–12).

In the duel almost at the conclusion of Thomas Mann's *The Magic Mountain* (published in 1924, but set over the seven years leading up to the First World War), Naphta shoots himself in the head after his opponent Settembrini, whom he had challenged, fires the first shot high into the mountains. It is not clear, though, that anyone regards this action as an exactly honour-restoring move. Duellistic imagery may be seen as one 'leitmotiv' running through the novel (in the Wagnerian sense acknowledged by Mann in his much later postscript essay, 'The Making of *The Magic Mountain*': Mann, 1996, 719–29, 725). This is particularly the case once Settembrini and Naphta begin their prolonged intellectual feuding in the second half of the work, the culmination of which is anticipated by the jotted account of a 'Polish *affaire d'honneur*' (ibid., 685–8). The eventual surprise (but fatal) duel itself here arises from intellectual affront rather than personal (let alone sexual) insult. The 'bombastic humanism' of a radical Freemason (the Italian, Settembrini) had long confronted the 'analphabetic barbarism' (523) of a 'Terrorist' Jesuit (Naphta: in fact of Jewish origin). And, in Settembrini's contention:

> The duel, my friend, is not an 'arrangement,' like another. It is the ultimate, the return to a state of nature, slightly mitigated by regulations which are chivalrous in character, but extremely superficial. The essential nature of the thing remains the primitive, the physical struggle; and however civilized a man is, it is his duty to be ready for such a contingency, which may any day arise. (699)

Mann, depicting in a symbolic fashion the institutions of these last European pre-war years, saw *The Magic Mountain* as 'the swan song of that form of existence' (721). In addition, the Settembrini–Naphta conflict may be regarded as a swan song not merely of dualism, but of literary duelling.

Both Mann and, a little earlier, Chekhov may have produced their intentional parodies of the duelling tradition (both historical and literary). However, there may also be a sense in which all duels may have been in any event, each with its own case and in its own way, a less intentional parody.

The slap in the face (*poshshechina*), a phenomenon, for whatever reason, particularly (though not exclusively – see Pitt-Rivers, 1965, 25) associated with Russian duelling and its surrounding causes and consequential actions, and one that remained of particular concern to Dostoevsky, survives the demise of duelling itself.[21] Among the post-Revolutionary Russian writers in whose fiction this motif occurs, we find the bizarre case of Daniil Kharms, whose minimalist tales are filled with all forms of mindless and unprovoked violence, 'in the best Dostoevskian tradition'; more recently, in Viacheslav P'etsukh's story *Duellists and I* (*Ia i duelianty*, 1990), 'the events leading to a duel are set in motion by a slap in the face' (Reyfman, 1999, 14). Boris Akunin's *The Winter Queen* (*Azazel'*, 1998), set back in 1876, features a duel orchestrated by means of dicing and Russian roulette (allegedly first known as 'American roulette').

*   *   *   *   *

> . . . prodded by a seminal idea: I felt like poisoning a monk.
> (Umberto Eco, *Reflections on The Name of the Rose*)

Monks have disported themselves in fiction in a wide variety of representations, as has been demonstrated in many of the works discussed above. In addition, of course, we meet our share of priests and confessors. Huysmans, in *The Damned*, unrolls a concatenation of 'rogue priests' whose purposes include the 'goal of unholy communion' or Black Mass, and the 'unbeneficed' (or 'loosely attached', to get rid of the troublesome) priests (see Huysmans, 2001, 54–6, 169). His protagonist Durtal even sees his cat as 'an inattentive and indulgent confessor' (ibid., 64). Although monks are mostly thought of as sojourning within monasteries, this is not always the case, and living as a monk may not necessarily be carried out literally (or within orders). Mann's Leverkühn, abandoning theology for music and indulging in 'confession in avoidance' (*DF*, 132), revels in 'intellectual monkishness' and 'monkish detachment' (*DF*, 210, 289). Zosima predicts, as a future for Alyosha Karamazov: 'you will leave these walls and will live in the world as a monk' (*KB*, 356 / *PSS*, 14, 259) – a state of existence noted by Thompson (1991, 234) as 'another hagiographical topos'.[22] Divisions exist between monastic orders and, for that matter, within any one order or within the same monastic walls: Fathers Ferapont and Paissy, in Dostoevsky's depiction, are contrasting and 'significant figures in the gallery of monks' (Jones, 2005, 116). Ferapont, indeed, is 'a fanatic', is 'strongly opposed to the institution of Elders' and is given to seeing little devils and to various other extremes of religious posturing (ibid.).

Monks did not, of course, always exist ('*Monasticism is man-made*': Hourihan, 2003, 71; italics in the original). Historically, if such it should be called, the religious identity of the monk is alleged to have formed through spiritual combat (or indeed duels) with demons in fourth- and fifth-century Egypt.[23] Such a chronology leads conveniently to the 'legend' featured in Chekhov's story *The Black Monk* (published in 1894) – the point of interest here, setting aside this story's concerns too with madness, music and the Gothic-style fall of a house and garden.[24]

Kovrin, the protagonist of this story, suddenly becomes obsessed with a legend, heard or read he knows not where (it having come to Chekhov himself in a dream). He relates to his companion Tanya:

> . . . A thousand years ago a black-garbed monk was walking through some Syrian or Arabian desert. A few miles away fishermen saw another black monk moving slowly over the surface of a lake. This second monk was a mirage. Now forget all the laws of optics seemingly ignored by the legend, and hear the next bit. The mirage generates another mirage. The second generates a third, and so the black monk's image

is endlessly transmitted from one atmospheric stratum to another. He is seen, now in Africa, now in Spain, now in India, now in the far north. Having left the earth's atmosphere behind at last, he now wanders through the entire universe, never encountering conditions which would enable him to fade away. Perhaps he's to be seen on Mars somewhere, now, or on some star of the Southern Cross. But the legend's very kernel and essence is this, my dear. Exactly a thousand years after that monk walked in the desert the mirage will return to the earth's atmosphere and manifest itself to men. The thousand years is said to be just about up, so we can expect the black monk any day now according to the legend. (Chekhov, 1989, 75 / Chekhov, 1962, 295)

The monk does indeed, and almost immediately, duly appear (at first hurtling past and subsequently entering into personal contact, being dubbed that 'unknown force': ibid., 94 / 319) – but only to Kovrin. In addition to his qualities, observed and confessed respectively as 'that optical incongruity' (81 / 303) and 'an apparition' ('*ia – prizrak*': 82 / 304), the black monk presents himself as somehow both spokesperson and recruiting agent for 'the Elect of God' and 'Eternal Truth' (ibid.).

In Ivan Karamazov's (unwritten but memorised) 'poem' (as Ivan terms it; commentators often refer to it as 'The Legend') of the Grand Inquisitor, it has been remarked: 'The Inquisitor is projected backwards 300 years in a quasi-fantastical setting inhabited by phantom figures' (Thompson, 1991, 304). After such Dostoevskian use of 'mystical symbolic dimension' (ibid.), and the Chekhovian virtual apotheosis, what further development could possibly be left to the monk in fiction? One answer remains parody. Indeed Chekhov's 'legend', as well as elements from Dostoevsky, is entertainingly played on much later in *Pelagia & The Black Monk* (2001), a novel by the writer of highly popular Russian historical detective fiction, Boris Akunin (the pseudonym of Grigory Chkhartishvili – making shameless play too with the Bakunin cognomenon).[25] There is a character called 'Alyosha'; a 'Father Zosima' is alluded to; there is no shortage of confession; an important bishop 'had served as a cavalry officer before he took monastic vows' (Akunin, 2007, 29); and the 'monkish' investigator is a cross-dressing nun.

One particular curiosity in this subgenre, in terms of both its origins and its content, is Ambrose Bierce's novella *The Monk and the Hangman's Daughter* (appearing from 1891 to 1906). Its final subtitle reveals it as 'written in collaboration with G.A. Danziger'; Danziger, however, had made 'a rough translation of Richard Voss's "Der Mönch von Berchtes-gaden"', purportedly based on 'an old manuscript originally belonging to the Franciscan monastery at Berchtesgaden, Bavaria' and obtained from a peasant (Bierce, 1960, 662–3). In its story, this work (the first-person narrative of a young monk named Ambrosius) contains a number of similarities, plus various opposites, as compared to the main stories out-lined above. There is confession and love interest, plus a duel (in the form of unarmed combat, in which it is the monk's life that is spared), and the whole is imbued with a series of injustices and misunderstandings stemming from sexual and religious fervour.

Monks and fierce priests have, of course, continued to appear in literature through the twentieth century and beyond, whether singly or in collective form. Savonarola, the feared Dominican friar, for example, makes appearances in period novels stretching at least from Dmitri Merezh-kovsky's *The Romance of Leonardo da Vinci* (1902) to Sarah Dunant's *The Birth of Venus* (2003) and Salman Rushdie's *The Enchantress of Florence* (2008), as well as inspiring the initial inspiration for Tom Wolfe's novel of American vani-ties, *The Bonfire of the Vanities* (1987). Rasputin, the 'Mad Monk', achieved cinematic status in Don Sharp's film titled under that phrase (in 1966).[26]

Yevgeny Zamyatin wrote mischievous monkish tales in Soviet Russia in the first half of the 1920s. An example of the solitary monk is Ervin (who has become the supposed miracle-working Father Severinus, in Gubbio, Italy) in Antal Szerb's *Journey by Moonlight* (1937: see the epigraph to the present chapter). In being a convert of Jewish origin, this figure resembles – in that respect, if in no other – Mann's Naphta. Ignazio Silone's *The Story of a Humble Christian* (1968) presents, in dramatic form, scenes and events following the Conclave of Perugia (of 1294). This includes (as well as such a concept as 'holy nihilism': Silone, 1970, 61) two popes. One is another extremely unworldly, childlike ecclesiastic, who becomes Celestine V, only to resign after three months, then to be known as Pier Celestine, dying in custody in 1296 – but then to achieve canonisation in 1313. His ruthless opponent and successor is Boniface VIII, and the work is, naturally enough, filled largely with further cardinals, friars and monks from the period following the Franciscan splits.[27] The opposition here between Boniface and Celestine seems almost reminiscent of that between Ivan Karamazov's Grand Inquisitor and Christ, or, for that matter, the ideological/theological opposition implied between Ivan himself and Zosima.

Umberto Eco's first novel, *The Name of the Rose* (1980), which may have plausible claims to being the great monk novel of the twentieth century, takes up almost as Silone's play leaves off. It is set in an unnamed abbey somewhere in northern Italy in 1327. The narrator, Adso of Melk (writing some sixty years later as 'this aging monk': Eco, 1984, 25), succinctly summarises the monastic situation in Italy from just before Saint Francis and over the years from Celestine and Boniface to another ruthless papal figure, John XXII (see ibid., 49–52). William of Baskerville (an English 'learned Franciscan', and a former inquisitor who had turned to Oxford studies), assisted by the Benedictine novice Adso, while on a mysterious diplomatic mission, is called upon to investigate a suspicious monastic death (soon becoming several) at the comfortable Benedictine abbey (boasting 'one hundred and fifty servants for sixty monks': 33).

Inspired by Roger Bacon, and an associate of William of Occam, William of Baskerville, as his name suggests, anachronistically anticipates the deductive methods to be used by Sherlock Holmes, and he finds his arch-antagonist in the blind fundamentalist librarian, Jorge of Burgos (a mischievous but affectionate play on Jorge Luis Borges).[28] Monks in Eco's novel have latrines, as well as dormitories and cells, and are susceptible to lusts of the flesh (much might hang on 'a quarrel between . . . between sodomite monks': 449). Heretics of many stripes vie with the respected or wavering ecclesiasticisms of the day; Minorites, Fraticelli and Spirituals are featured, with references going back even to the monks of Hibernia and Ultima Thule. Laughter is seen by Jorge as the most serious danger to spirituality and the fear of death: Aristotle's lost theory of comedy must be suppressed at all costs. In the end, of course, it is, as 'the detective is defeated' (54). In the 'duel' between William and Jorge, moreover, allusion has been noticed to the dialogues between Naptha and Settembrini (Eco, 2006, 125).[29]

Adso's reliving his own story as an old man takes the 'fundamental' model of its mode of narration from Mann's *Doctor Faustus* (ibid.; and Eco, 1984, 33). Adso, even as a young man, comes to realise that, to monks and laymen, 'not infrequently books speak of books' and a monastic library can seem 'all the more disturbing' a place (Eco, 1984, 286) – and eventually a deadly one. He knows, as does the reader, that 'the one thing that frightens us' is 'the metaphysical shudder' (ibid., 53).

If *The Name of the Rose* is the monk novel of the twentieth century, Thomas Merton was, allegedly, 'the most photographed monk of the century' (Hourihan, 2003, 12). Paul Hourihan's *The Death of Thomas Merton* (2003) is subtitled 'A Novel', and it bears the further extended subtitle (on cover and title page) of 'A Confessional Portrayal of the Last Day in the Life of the Famous Catholic Monk and Writer'. We have here then both monk and confession, though not exactly duel – although a familiar dualistic conflict is carried on between various pairs of concepts: West and East, the Catholic and the Vedantic,[30] the inward and the outward, verbalisation and mysticism (the literary and the spiritual). Other minor contradictions include Trappism versus loquacity, monasticism and lust, 'Tom Merton, modern seer' (ibid., 22) and yet 'not a seer' (102). The confessional meditation, largely in stream of consciousness form, is carried out in first, second and third persons (giving rise to what might be considered 'telepathy' in more than one sense – including that, noted earlier, used by Nicholas Royle in his 2003 study *The uncanny*). His writing career now dismissed as 'glib fluency' (Hourihan, 2003, 30), Merton, with his (to himself at least) insufferable ego, is 'a prophet who had become a bore', who 'would spoil everything by living longer' (ibid., 136). His confession (at times 'a kind of erotic confessional': 33) becomes a trial and an indictment. His crisis of faith ('in a post-Christian world': 49) is severe, and faith in any case is reduced now to preservation 'from mischief and despair' (138).

Alon Hilu's *Death of a Monk* (published in Hebrew in 2004) has the historical setting of the Damascus Blood Libel of 1840, as a result of which the Jewish population narrowly escaped a drastic fate, following false accusations regarding the murder of a monk and his manservant for ritual purposes. The historical events, and all the central characters, were real (see Hilu's 'Postscript'); the circumstances and personal details are fictionalised. Father Tomaso, a badly behaving elderly Capuchin monk from Sardinia, who operates largely as a 'junk merchant' around Damascus (Hilu, 2006, 94), inadvertently sets events in train by perishing while engaged in the anal penetration of the novel's young Jewish protagonist and narrator, Aslan.[31] However, it is Aslan's ruthlessness, combined with his utter incompetence, which leads, in the wake of what has happened (the 'trifling matter' of 'the disappearance of a sinful monk' (ibid., 105)), to the brink of communal disaster – the day being saved only by 'near-miraculous' international intervention.

Aslan's false accusations come at a critical stage of what has been in effect a long-standing duel with his family, and indeed with Judaism itself – sparring almost from birth: over abuse, neglect and sexuality. Without suggesting that this novel is derivative as such (its historical legitimacy guards adequately enough against that, not to mention its individualistic flourishes), we can still see it as an appropriate conclusion to the sequence of monkish novels here traced. Aslan's attempts at parricide (his accusations all but bring about the execution of his father, his father in law and two uncles – a third dies anyway under mistreatment) recall the Karamazov family. The advance of a plague in Damascus recalls Manzoni's Milan. The emanation of the narrative from an 'arid mountain' (Mount Lebanon), awaiting the visit of a 'doctor-priest' (300) may suggest (if in part by atmospheric contrast) Thomas Mann. Moreover, the narrative method (the confessional story recited by an aged monk, for transcription by his novice-'foundling') prompts recollection of Zosima and Alyosha, plus, with the timescale (of almost sixty years), the narrative structure employed in *The Name of the Rose*. Finally, we have met already Christian monks of Jewish origin: Aslan here makes his final familial and religious break by confessional conversion. As well as highlighting the highly sensational death of a monk, Hilu's novel engages, in consequence, with the birth of a monk.

*   *   *   *   *

Confession, in a variety of forms, has been much in evidence throughout the history of literary writings (fictional or otherwise – assuming such a difference is demonstrable), with obvious key examples stemming from works by Saint Augustine and Rousseau. From Rousseau, Northrop Frye points out, 'the confession flows into the novel' (Frye, 1971,

307). Again, Dostoevsky is seen as an apex in this, as in various other forms of writing.[32] Russian writings include Karamzin's fictional *My Confession* (*Moia ispoved'*, 1802) and Tolstoy's non-fictional *A Confession* (*Ispoved'*, written – too late for Dostoevsky's purposes – in 1879–81, and first published in Geneva in 1884), a work which contributed towards his eventual excommunication from the Orthodox Church.[33] Dostoevsky is known to have read confession-titled fiction by George Sand and Alfred de Musset, along with other European works exploiting this form of discourse, and may have gained monastic insights from his younger friend, the poet and religious thinker Vladimir Solov'ev (Solovyov), assumed to be a part model for Alyosha Karamazov.[34] From the Dostoevskian *oeuvre*, preceding his final novel, reference is frequently made in confessional regard to the *Notes from Underground* and to Stavrogin's 'Confession', the chapter omitted by the censorship from *The Devils* (*Besy*) – though many a further Dostoevsky text remains open to, and does indeed receive, such discussion.[35]

Michael Holquist (1986, 170) interprets Georg Lukács as being largely concerned (in his Hegelian *The Theory of the Novel*, 1920) with 'the biography/confession opposition'. Frye makes the obvious link between confession and autobiography, mentioning also the *Künstler-roman* and the 'stream of consciousness' technique (see Frye, 1971, 307–8, 312–14). Michel Foucault (1981, 20) has noted the transformation of, in particular, sex into discourse, devised long ago 'in an ascetic and monastic setting'. And, indeed, the very opposite can feature too in literary works by the decadents, such as Huysmans and Mendès.[36] Confession as ritual for 'the production of truth' was codified, as a sacrament of penance, by the Lateran Council in 1215, 'with the resulting development of confessional techniques' (Foucault, 1981, 58). This process invaded 'justice, medicine, education, family relationships, and love relations' – extending from 'the most ordinary affairs of everyday life' to 'the most solemn rites' (ibid., 59). Every desire is transformed into discourse, and this practise in due course enters literature (taken up for instance by de Sade). Violence, or its threat (whether in this world or the next) shadows the process, and indeed the coupling of torture with confession was to be found back in Greek and Roman law (59, n. 2).[37] Huysmans, in *The Damned*, relating the fifteenth-century case of Gilles de Rais, cites ecclesiastical law as stating that 'a confession cannot be regarded as evidence if it is "*dubia, vaga, generalis illativa, jocosa*"' – requiring that the accused be subjected to the 'canonic question', meaning torture.[38]

In his Bakhtinian study *Confession in the Novel*, Les W. Smith notes that, in developing his theory of the novel, and his concept of dialogism in particular, 'Bakhtin draws on narratological strategies innate to the practice of religious confession' (Smith, 1996, 31). 'Confessants', apparently, 'never overcome their sense of incompleteness', causing a never concluded 'inherent conflict between narrative strategies' (ibid., 32). An analogy emerges 'between confession and fiction', with a perspective similar to that holding true 'between author and character' (33). Confession can thus resemble 'an aesthetic act, where perpetual conflict between author and hero shapes narrative' – 'just as the confrontation between self and other shapes confession' (34). In Dostoevsky's *The Double* (*Dvoinik*), to take a prominent early example, it is argued: 'Author and character find themselves locked in reflective relations with each other, just as Golyadkin is with his double and other characters' (57). Smith discusses this work, followed by *Notes from Underground* (*Zapiski iz podpol'ia*), before proceeding to questions Karamazovian.

What is seen as important here in particular, is a distinction between 'confession *of*' and 'confession *that*' (see Smith, 1996, 31–2, 67–8), at the same time interlinking *chronos* and *kairos*. The former is fragmented and digressive, while the latter necessitates an external dimension (32). 'Confession *of*' is recognised in the utterances of Fyodor Karamazov and his sons, as in the discourse of the Underground Man, following the 'self-assertive rhetoric' of Rousseau (involving much 'deceitful posturing': 67, 69). 'Confession *that*', on the other hand, 'represented by Zosima and other monks', is 'more like Saint Augustine in his *Confessions*' (67). The former type, found too in the story of the Grand Inquisitor (another 'metaphysical centre' to the novel: Miller, 1990, 106), leading to implosion, is balanced by, interacts with or responds to the latter (as in, say, 'the hagiographic account of Zosima's life'), with its consequence of novelistic transcendence (Smith, 1996, 82–3). Zosima, highlighted as 'A Russian Monk' (the title of Book Six) has, as a counterweight, 'that Western Monk, the Grand Inquisitor' (Hackel, 1983, 165).[39] The *pro* and *contra* theme is anyway made explicit in the title of Book Five ('*Pro* i *contra*' / 'Pros and Cons').

Belknap (1990a) provides alternative variations in his essay 'The Unrepentant Confession', as contrasted with repentant or less than totally repentant examples of the phenomenon. A prime example to stress here, from the Gothic period, would be James Hogg's *The Private Memoirs and Confessions of a Justified Sinner* (1824). Smith, for his part, goes on to examine forms of confession in three twentieth-century works: Mauriac's *Thérèse Desqueyroux* (1927) and its sequels, Flannery O'Connor's *Wise Blood* (1952) and Don DeLillo's *Mao II* (1991). No doubt further examples and developments could be adduced. False confession, amounting in consequence to unbridled accusation, plays its part in Hilu's *Death of a Monk*.

In addition to imagery of the duel in *The Magic Mountain*, in that novel can also be found leitmotifs of monastic existence and confession.[40] Monastic and monkish imagery (see, for example, Mann, 1968, 194) foreshadows the appearance of Naphta – associated with the 'monkish tradition' (ibid., 377) although, by reason of illness, he has not become a fully fledged member of the Jesuit order. A later character, Mynheer Peeperkorn, is identified with 'the ritual impropriety of the heathen priest' (621). There are references to 'confessional flogging' (455) and arguments involving the Inquisition, confession and torture as 'a madness of asceticism' (459–60). At least equally notable is the introduction of the natural successor to confession, namely psychoanalysis, practised somewhat controversially (according to some, at any rate) at the Berghof international sanatorium by Dr Krokowski (9). This specialist lectures and gesticulates 'like Christ on the cross' (130) and is dubbed by Settembrini 'the father-confessor' indulging in 'papish practices' (96). Even the novel's main (and mostly secular) protagonist, Hans Castorp, when in Samaritan mode, will visit and counsel the more seriously sick 'in a physicianly and priestly capacity' (303). The disputes which lead eventually (if improbably) to the final duel, interlink and interact in much the same manner analysed above through the 'confession *of*' and 'confession *that*' dichotomy. These disputes confront and convolute, among other dualities, the Inquisition with the Jacobins, scholasticism with humanism, 'obedience' with 'freedom', Augustine with Rousseau and 'faith' with 'illusion'.[41] The upshot, in similar fashion, produces implosion and explosion, in the form of, successively, a transcendental and a suicidal shot.

*   *   *   *   *

The present chapter, then (as was noted at its commencement), suggests that the featured narratives by Odoevsky and Manzoni may be seen as models which Dostoevsky must have known, and is likely to have had in mind for play or variation. Manzoni, as far as I have discovered, has barely entered the lists of Dostoevsky scholarship (although it would be surprising if no such connection has been noted or proposed by Italian Slavists[42]). In the case of Odoevsky's *The Witness*, however, the similarity – what he calls a striking example of 'pure confluence' – *has* been remarked: in a note to an essay published in 1968 by Claude Backvis (see Backvis, 1968, 549–50; noted subsequently in

Cornwell, 1986, 55). Odoevsky's ambitious and unrealised poetic-dramatic 'mystery' of the 1830s, 'Segeliel': A Don Quixote of the 19th Century', was to have combined a well-intentioned fallen-angel protagonist (perhaps contributing towards Dostoevsky's *The Idiot*), otherworld qualities (*dvoemirie*), alchemy and a posited duel (with Lucifer to act as second).[43] Various 'real life' models for Dostoevsky's Zosima and his teachings, as well as other monks, have been put forward (see Grigorieff, 1967; Terras, 1981, 29–30; Hackel, 1983; Linnér, 1975). From these, however, the nearest we get to the particular biographical concerns of the present chapter appears to be the intelligence (from Grigorieff, 1967, 25–6) that one spiritual teacher of one (possibly prime) model had been 'a dashing cavalry officer before taking monastic vows'.

These last remarks form something of a conclusion to Chapter 4. As well as appending a brief further conclusion to the study as a whole, we offer, as an appendix, the two previously mentioned first translations of stories by Vladimir Odoevsky, the author whose works supplied the initial impulses for the four chapters of this book.

Notes

1 Although this novel has been more customarily known as *The Brothers Karamazov*, it is hard to disagree with Ignat Avsey, translator of the version used here, that, had they not slavishly followed the word order of the original title (*Brat'ia Karamazovy*), previous translators 'would no more have dreamt of saying The Brothers Karamazov than they would The Brothers Warner or The Brothers Marx' (*KB*, xxx). Page numbers in this novel are cited from Avsey's translation (OUP, 1994, 1998; abbreviated as *KB*), followed by those from the *Polnoe sobranie sochinenii*, vols 14 and 15 (Leningrad: Nauka, 1976; shortened to *PSS*).

2 'Schemahieromonk' (*Ieroskhimonakh*): a rarer status of monk, under a stricter order of monastic discipline than the more

normal 'hieromonk' (*ieromonakh*) – a priest in a monastic order, as opposed to a lay brother (*KB*, 995; *Oxford Russian Dictionary*, 3rd edn, 2000).

3 On the narrator in *The Karamazov Brothers*, see Terras (1981, 87–90) and Thompson (1991, 26–51). The *starets* phenomenon is a feature of Eastern Orthodoxy, disputed within Russian Orthodoxy, the 'Elder' being one who subsumes the soul of his adherents, to deliver a kind of guru guidance (see *KB*, 34–5 and elsewhere; *PSS*, 14, 26–7).

4 See W.J. Mc Cormack's introduction to his (1985) edition of the work, exploring its context within Le Fanu's *oeuvre* and his treatment of the Manzoni connection.

5 Page references are to the Russian edition (1959); the translation is my own (previously unpublished: see Appendix).

6 In one sense the title *The Italian* appears bizarre. It seemingly relates to the principal villainous figure, that of 'father Schedoni, an Italian, as his name imported' (Radcliffe, 1987, 34); with the exception of the English travellers appearing in the prologue, the entire cast of the novel (unsurprisingly, given its setting) is Italian.

7 Victor Brombert, *The Romantic Prison: The French Tradition*, Princeton, NJ: Princeton University Press, 1978, p. 150 (see 'Huysmans: The Prison House of Decadence', pp. 150–70).

8 Scaruffi, 2003, p. 281. This dissertation, 'My Body is a Room from Which I Cannot Escape', compares the phenomenon of the *studiolo* (of Federico da Montefeltro at his palaces in Gubbio and Urbino) with Odoevsky's study (in both reality and his fiction), as well as examining, in relation to Odoevsky's *Russian Nights*, Castiglione's *The Book of the Courtier*, the works of Piranesi and the writings of Jeremy Bentham.

9 On this and related themes, see *Italy and the Gothic*, ed. Massimiliano Demata, special issue of *Gothic Studies*, (8, 1 May 2006), esp. Demata's introduction (pp. 1–8).

10 Quoted from 'John Moore, Ann Radcliffe and the Gothic Vision of Italy', in Demata, ed., *Italy and the Gothic*, pp. 35–51 (pp. 37, 39).

11 Robin Milner-Gulland, discussion point during Neo-Formalist Circle conference, Oxford, 1999.

12 See similar comments, on 'Chinese boxes', reported in Robin F. Miller's essay on the two works (1990).

13 Gait (whether 'monastic' or 'jaunty') seems to be a matter of some concern regarding monks: '[Thomas] Merton's *boisterous walk* is alone enough to exclude him from spiritual light' (Hourihan, 2003, 124; original italics).

14 See however the recent study by Richard Hopton, *Pistols at Dawn: A History of Duelling*, London: Portrait, 2007.

15 As a comment on duelling, Tom Stoppard, in *Voyage* (the first part of his dramatic trilogy *The Coast of Utopia*, 2002), has Turgenev say, in contrast to the death from tuberculosis of Nikolai Stankevich: 'Beside it, Pushkin's death is a comedy . . . An absurdity. If we weren't in tears it would be side-splitting. No other social class but ours could count it natural behaviour, to march grimly into the snow with loaded pistols and bang away because according to some anonymous lampoon a woman who once stirred your blood, and now only irritates you, is being kept occupied by someone as yet in the first stage of discovery. If we lived somewhere like . . . the Sandwich Islands it would be the seducer who gets the sniggers while the husband hands out cigars to his friends'. Tom Stoppard, *The Coast of Utopia: Voyage, Shipwreck, Salvage* (London: Faber, 2008), 54.

16 The activity of the *bretteur* (*Fr.*): duellist or swashbuckler.

17 One of Bestuzhev-Marlinsky's tales, *The Terrible Divination* (*Strashnoe gadanie*, 1830), includes too the visit (in a Yuletide dream) of a 'mysterious stranger' (the devil).

18 See Tulloch (1980, 117–31) and Rayfield (1999, 101–7) for analyses of Chekhov's *The Duel*.

19 See *The Dedalus Book of Russian Decadence: Perversity, Despair and Collapse*, ed. Kirsten Lodge, Sawtry, Cambs.: Dedalus, 2007, pp. 199–217 (210).

20 A. Kobrinskii, *Duel'nye istorii Serebrianogo veka. Poedinki poetov kak fakt literaturnoi zhizni. Duel'nyi kodeks*, St Petersburg: Vita Nova, 2007.

21 Reyfman considers the slap in the face in the light of the New Testament (228) and refers to Pascal's Christian criticism of duelling and, indeed, the slap in the face (1999, 338, n. 80).

22 Dostoevsky (*PSS*, 14, 259) uses here the alternative Russian work *inok*, rather than the more customary *monakh*.

23 See Alastair Sooke, 'The Hot Club', *TLS*, 15 Dec. 2006, p. 8, reviewing demonic studies, including David Brakke, *Demons*

and the Making of the Monk, Cambridge, MA: Harvard University Press, 2006.

24 See Ann Komaromi's analysis of this work (1999); and, on it and music, Rayfield (1999, 128), plus remarks noted in the opening chapter.

25 However, whichever may have been the primary intention, 'Akunin' is also said to be 'a pseudonym from a Japanese word that loosely translates as villain': Luke Harding, 'Move over Tolstoy: Detective Tales of Tsarist Era Take Russia by Storm', *Guardian*, 19 Sep. 2007, p. 25 (reporting on the popularity of the Erast Fandorin novels).

26 The lengthy historical novel by Valentin Pikul', *U poslednei cherty* ('At the End of the Line', 1979), in which Rasputin features, and which was reissued as *Nechistaia sila* ('Evil Spirit', 1991), appears not to have been translated.

27 On the possible presence of Celestine V in Dante's *Inferno* (Canto 3), blamed as the man who from cowardice made 'the grand refusal' (*il gran rifiuto*), see Silone, 1970, 204.

28 On the significance of Bacon and Occam, see Eco, 1985, 26; while, for Eco, 'library plus blind man can only equal Borges' (28). For Eco's appreciation of Borges, see his essay in *On Literature* (118–35).

29 Eco (1985, 30) refers also to the model of '*The Magic Mountain*, with its mountainous, sanative situation, where so many conversations could take place'.

30 Vedanta (end of the Veda): an orthodox system of Hindu philosophy developing in a qualified monism the speculations of the Upanishads on ultimate reality and the liberation of the soul (Webster's *New Collegiate Dictionary*).

31 Well before the activities written of in the novels of Eco and Hilu, Huysmans, in his *The Damned* (1891), had conjured with a form of 'Divine sodomy, so to speak': 'priests, in their baseness' celebrating 'the Mass with great hosts, which they then pierce through the middle and glue to a parchment . . . and this they do use abominably and to satisfy their passions' (Huysmans, 2001, 60).

32 On Dostoevsky and Rousseau, with specific reference to the former's *Notes from Underground*, see Howard's article (1981); Miller (1984), on various texts; and Belknap, 'The Unrepentant Confession' (1990a), which considers *Notes*, plus Fedor Karamazov's confession.

33 For common and compatible 'confessional' reasons, Tolstoy's
    A Confession is coupled with Dostoevsky's *Notes from Under-
    ground* in the Everyman Library edition, ed. A.D.P. Briggs
    (London: J.M. Dent, 1994) – 'each in its own way a *tour de force*
    of rhetorical discourse' (introd., xxv).
34 On Dostoevsky's reading, see Belknap 1990b, ch. 2:
    'Dostoevsky Read Enormously . . .' (pp. 15–44).
35 See Terekhova's M. Litt. thesis (2007) on this topic, noting the
    critics who have examined it. What is more, Dostoevsky's last
    novel, according to Terekhova (2), provides the 'only oppor-
    tunity' for a full analysis of the phenomenon of confession (in
    what are taken as its three forms: the religious, the judicial and
    the literary) within the framework of a single work.
36 See the references to the conjoining of confession with sex
    (or the turning of confession into sex) in Huysmans, *The
    Damned* (2001). A short story by Catulle Mendès, 'The Peni-
    tent' (*La Pénitente*, of the mid-1880s), depicts a seductive
    female causing a priest to faint in the confession-box: trans.
    The Dedalus Book of French Horror: The 19ᵗʰ Century, ed. Terry
    Hale, Sawtry, Cambs.: Dedalus, 1998, pp. 167–71.
37 See Foucault on confession: 1981, 18–22, 57–73. Belknap
    (1990a, 117), while noting Foucault's suggestion that 'con-
    fession may have become a dominant mode of communication
    in our culture over the last few centuries', proposes that 'in the
    recent expressionist decades, the self-justifying apologia may
    well have overtaken it'.
38 'Unclear, confused, unspecific, partial, in jest' (Huysmans,
    2001, 210, 276 n.).
39 On possible sources shaping Dostoevsky's Grand Inquisitor,
    see Belknap, 1990b, 111–25. An apparently fictional 'source',
    mischievously proposed in a recent novel, is *Le grand pasha*, by
    one Dr Ferit Kemal (a Turkish author writing in French), sup-
    posedly published in Paris in 1870: Ohan Pamuk, *The Black
    Book* (*Kara Kitap*, 1990), trans. Maureen Freely, London:
    Faber, 2006, 153. Pamuk may be responding to the inclusion
    in Dostoevsky's novel of an apparently frivolous reference
    to *Muhammad's Kinsman or Curative Foolery* (*Rodstvennik
    Magometa, ili Tsenitol'noe durachestvo*) (685 / 14, 493): a trans-
    lation from the French, published in Moscow in 1785, recount-
    ing the amorous adventures of a Frenchman in Constantinople

(see 1002 / 15, 581). There are also negative references to Islam (noted by Jones, 2005, 152).

40 Thomas Mann proceeds further into a more entertaining confessional mode in *Confessions of Felix Krull, Confidence Man* (begun in 1910 and published, as his last novel, in 1954).

41 On this last duality, see Jones (2005, 153), who bases much of his reading on Mikhail Epstein's concept of 'minimal religion' – oppositions of 'alternative' religious views, from varieties of faith to nihilism, stemming possibly from 'apophatic theology' (see Jones, 2005, *passim*, and Conclusion, 147–54). Readers of Huysmans might want to add, along with him (52), Manicheism: 'The Principle of Good and the Principle of Evil, the God of Light and the God of Darkness, two rivals fighting over our souls'.

42 The one instance I have so far traced deals with another text (by Enrichetta Caracciolo, translated into French, English and German in the 1860s) of shared interest to Dostoevsky and Manzoni, rather than any knowledge Dostoevsky may have had of Manzoni: Bruno Basile, 'Dostoevskij, Manzoni e '/ *Misteri del Chiostro Napoletano*"', *Lettere italiane*, 38, 2 (1986), 233–41.

43 See Koren'kov, 2007; and Cornwell, 1986, 63–4.

References and further reading

Primary sources

Akunin, Boris, 2007, *Pelagia & The Black Monk* (*Pelagiia i chernyi monakh*, 2001), trans. Andrew Bromfield, London: Weidenfeld & Nicolson.

Bierce, Ambrose, *The Monk and the Hangman's Daughter*, 1960, *The Collected Writings of Ambrose*, with an introduction by Clifton Fadiman, New York: The Citadel Press, pp. 661–724.

Castiglione, Baldesar, [1967] 1976, *The Book of the Courtier* (*Il Cortegiano*, 1528), trans. George Bull, London: Penguin Books.

Castiglione, Count Baldassare, [1974] 1994, *The Book of the Courtier*, ed. Virginia Cox, London: Everyman [the Hoby translation, orig. *The Courtyer*, 1561].

Chekhov, A.P., 1962, 'Chernyi monakh'. A.P. Chekhov, *Sobranie sochinenii v dvenadtsati tomakh*, Moscow: Gos. izdat. Khudozhestvennoi literatury, vol. 7, pp. 288–321.

Chekhov, A.P., 1962, 'Duel' &. A.P. Chekhov, *Sobranie sochinenii v dvenadtsati tomakh*, Moscow: Gos. izdat. Khudozhestvennoi literatury, vol. 6, pp. 379–488.

Chekhov, Anton, 1989, 'The Black Monk'. Anton Chekhov, *A Woman's Kingdom and other Stories*, trans. Ronald Hingley, Oxford: Oxford University Press, pp. 70–96.

Chekhov, Anton, 1994, 'The Duel', *The Chekhov Omnibus: Selected Stories*, trans. Constance Garnett, rev. and ed. Donald Rayfield, London: Everyman, pp. 134–221.

Chekhov, Anton, 1995, *The Black Monk and Peasants*, trans. Ronald Wilks, London: Penguin (Penguin 60s), (translation of 'The Black Monk' first published in *The Kiss and Other Stories*, 1984).

Dostoevsky, F.M., 1976, *Brat'ia Karamazovy*. F.M. Dostoevsky, *Polnoe sobranie sochinenii v tridtsati tomakh*, vols 14 and 15, Leningrad: Nauka.

Dostoevsky, Fyodor, [1994] 1998, *The Karamazov Brothers*, trans. Ignat Avsey, Oxford: Oxford University Press.

Dostoyevsky, Fyodor, 1994, *Notes from Underground* and Lev Tolstoy, *A Confession*, ed. A.D.P. Briggs, London: Everyman.

Eco, Umberto, 1984, *The Name of the Rose* (*Il nome della rosa*, 1980), trans. William Weaver, London: Picador.

Hilu, Alon, 2006, *Death of a Monk* (*Mot Ha-Nazir*, 2004), trans. Evan Fallenberg, London: Harvill Secker.

Hoffmann, E.T.A., 1963, *The Devil's Elixirs* (*Die Elixiere des Teufels*, 1816), trans. Ronald Taylor, London: John Calder, 1963; repr. Richmond: Oneworld Classics, 2009.

Hourihan, Paul, 2003, *The Death of Thomas Merton: A Novel*, Redding, CA: Vedantic Shores Press.

Huysmans, J.-K., 2001, *The Damned (Là-Bas)*, trans. Terry Hale, Harmondsworth: Penguin.

Le Fanu, J. Sheridan, 1985, *Borrhomeo the Astrologer: A Monkish Tale*, introd. W.J. Mc Cormack, Edinburgh: The Tragara Press.

Lewis, Matthew G., 1959, *The Monk*, New York: Grove Press.

Mann, Thomas, [1927] 1996, *The Magic Mountain* (*Der Zauerberg*, 1924), trans. H.T. Lowe-Porter, London: Minerva.

Mann, Thomas, [1949] 1968, *Doctor Faustus: The Life of the German Composer Adrian Leverkühn as told by a friend* (*Doktor*

Faustus. Das Leben des deutschen Tonsetzers Adrian Leverkühn, erzählt von einem Freunde, 1947), trans. H.T. Lowe-Porter, Harmondsworth: Penguin.

Manzoni, Alessandro, 1972, *The Betrothed*, trans. Bruce Penman, Harmondsworth: Penguin.

Manzoni, Alessandro, 2002, *I Promessi Sposi*, vol. 1 (1827), Milan: Arnaldo Mondadori.

Maturin, Charles, 1977, *Melmoth the Wanderer: A Tale*, ed. Alethea Hayter, Harmondsworth: Penguin.

Nabokov, Vladimir, 1969, *Speak, Memory*, Harmondsworth: Penguin.

Nabokov, Vladimir, [1964; rev. 1975] 1990, *Eugene Onegin: A Novel in Verse by Aleksandr Pushkin*, trans. with commentary and index by Vladimir Nabokov, 2nd Princeton/Bollingen pbk edn.

Nabokov, Vladimir, [1941] 1995, *The Real Life of Sebastian Knight*, afterword by John Lanchester, Harmondsworth: Penguin.

Odoevsky, V.F., 1959, 'Svidetel'', in V.F. Odoevsky, *Povesti i rasskazy*, Moscow: Gos. izdat. Khudozhestvennoi literatury, pp. 332–41.

Radcliffe, Ann, [1981] 1987, *The Italian or the Confessional of the Black Penitents*, ed. and introd. Frederiek Garber, Oxford: Oxford University Press.

Silone, Ignazio, 1970, *The Story of a Humble Christian* (*L'avventura di un povero cristiano*, 1968), trans. William Weaver, New York: Harper & Row.

Szerb, Antal, [2001] 2006, *Journey by Moonlight* (*Utas és Holdvilág*, Budapest, 1937), trans. Len Rix, London: Pushkin Press.

Secondary sources

Anglo, Sydney, 2000, *The Martial Arts of Renaissance Europe*, New Haven and London: Yale University Press.

Backvis, Claude, 1968, 'Trois notes sur l'oeuvre littéraire du prince Vladimir Odoevskij', *AIPS* (Brussels), 19, pp. 517–97.

Belknap, Robert L., 1990a, 'The Unrepentant Confession', in Robert L. Belknap, ed. *Russianness: Studies on a Nation's Identity. In Honor of Rufus Mathewson, 1918–1970*, Ann Arbor: Ardis, pp. 113–23.

Belknap, Robert L., 1990b, *The Genesis of The Brothers Karamazov: The Aesthetics, Ideology, and Psychology Text Making*, Evanston,

IL: Northwestern University Press, Studies of the Harriman Institute.

Blackall, Eric A., 1983, 'The Divided Self: Hoffmann', in his *The Novels of the German Romantics*, Ithaca and London: Cornell University Press, pp. 221–41.

Butler, Elizabeth M., [1952] 1998, *The Fortunes of Faust*, Stroud, Glos.: Sutton Publishing; 'The First Faust Reborn, 1947', pp. 321–38.

Cornwell, Neil, 1986, *The Life, Times and Milieu of V.F. Odoyevsky, 1804–1869*, with a Foreword by Sir Isaiah Berlin. London: Athlone Press and Athens, OH: Ohio University Press.

Eco, Umberto, 1985, *Reflections on The Name of the Rose* (*Postille a Il nome della rosa*, 1983), trans. William Weaver, London: Secker & Warburg.

Eco, Umberto, 2006, 'Borges and My Anxiety of Influence', in his *On Literature* (*Sulla Letteratura*, 2002), trans. Martin McLaughlin, London: Vintage. pp. 118–35.

Foucault, Michel, 1981, *The History of Sexuality. Volume One: An Introduction* (*La Volonté de savoir*, 1976), trans. Robert Hurley, Harmondsworth: Penguin.

Frye, Northrop, [1957] 1971, *Anatomy of Criticism: Four Essays*, Princeton, NJ: Princeton University Press.

Grigorieff, Dmitry F., 1967, 'Dostoevsky's Elder Zosima and the Real Life of Father Amvrosy', *Vladimir's Seminary Quarterly*, 11, pp. 22–34.

Hackel, Sergei, 1983, 'The Religious Dimension: Vision or Evasion? Zosima's Discourse in *The Brothers Karamazov*', in Malcolm V. Jones and Garth M. Terry, eds, *New Essays on Dostoyevsky*, Cambridge: Cambridge University Press, pp. 139–68.

Holquist, Michael, 1986, *Dostoevsky and the Novel*, Evanston, IL: Northwestern University Press.

Howard, Barbara F., 1981, 'The Rhetoric of Confession: Dostoevskij's *Notes from Underground* and Rousseau's *Confessions*', *Slavic and East European Journal*, 25, 4, pp. 16–32.

Jones, Malcolm, 2005, *Dostoevsky and the Dynamics of Religious Experience*, London: Anthem Press.

Komaromi, Ann, 1999, 'Unknown Force: Gothic Realism in Chekhov's *The Black Monk*', in Neil Cornwell, ed. *The Gothic-Fantastic in Nineteenth-Century Russian Literature*, Amsterdam and Atlanta, GA: Rodopi, pp. 257–75.

Koren'kov, A.V., 2007, 'Paralleli romana F.M. Dostoevskogo "Idiot" i misterii V.F. Odoevskogo "Segeliel"', in *Dostojevskij a dnešok* (ed. Natália Muránska), Nitra, pp. 201–16.

Leatherbarrow, W.J., 1992, *Fyodor Dostoyevsky: The Brothers Karamazov*, Cambridge: Cambridge University Press.

Linnér, Sven, 1975, *Starets Zosima in 'The Brothers Karamazov': A Study in the Mimesis of Virtue*, Stockholm: Almqvist & Wiksell.

Miller, Robin Feuer, 1984, 'Dostoevsky and Rousseau: The Morality of Confession', in Robert Louis Jackson, ed. *Dostoevsky: New Perspectives*, Englewood Cliffs, NJ: Prentice-Hall, pp. 82–98.

Miller, Robin Feuer, 1990, 'The Metaphysical Novel and the Evocation of Anxiety: *Melmoth the Wanderer* and *The Brothers Karamazov*, A Case Study', in Robert L. Belknap, ed. *Russianness: Studies on a Nation's Identity. In Honor of Rufus Mathewson, 1918–1970*, Ann Arbor: Ardis, pp. 94–112.

Pitt-Rivers, Julian, 1965, 'Honour and Social Status', in J.G. Peristiany, ed. *Honour and Shame: The Values of Mediterranean Society*, London: Weidenfeld and Nicolson, pp. 19–77.

Rayfield, Donald, 1999, *Understanding Chekhov: A Critical Study of Chekhov's Prose and Drama*, London: Bristol Classical Press.

Reyfman, Irina, 1999, *Ritualized Violence Russian Style: The Duel in Russian Culture and Literature*, Stanford, CA: Stanford University Press.

Royle, Nicholas, 2003, *The uncanny*, Manchester: Manchester University Press.

Scaruffi, Ellen, 2003, 'My Body is a Room from Which I Cannot Escape: The Metaphysical Prisons of Prince Vladimir Odoevsky', PhD thesis, Columbia University.

Smith, Les W., 1996, *Confession in the Novel: Bakhtin's Author Revisited*, Madison, WI: Fairleigh Dickinson University Press.

Terekhova, Irina, 2007, 'Confessionalism of Dostoesvksy's *The Brothers Karamazov*' (Ispovedal'nost' 'Brat'ev Karamazovykh' F.M. Dostoevskogo), M.Litt. thesis, University of Bristol.

Terras, Victor, 1981, *A Karamazov Companion*, Madison, WI: University of Wisconsin Press.

Thompson, Diane Oenning, 1991, *The Brothers Karamazov and the Poetics of Memory*, Cambridge: Cambridge University Press.

Tulloch, John, 1980, *Chekhov: A Structuralist Study*, London and Basingstoke: Macmillan.

Conclusion

> We confused France with her literature. And true literature
> was that magic, a word, a verse, a chapter of which trans-
> ported us into a changeless moment of beauty.
>
> (Andreï Makine, *Le Testament français*)[1]

As a conclusion to this volume, we shall just look briefly at
some of the 'pathways' within, and to, a fairly recent prize-
winning novel, published in 1995 and written by a Russian,
Andreï Makine (born in 1957), who writes only in French
and has been resident in France since 1987.

A curiously bi-cultural novel, of a pseudo-autobiograph-
ical nature, *Le Testament français* (complete with capitals in
the English-translation titular rendering of its original
French title) contains at least traces of the pathways explored
in the present study. It also includes, of course, striking features of its own, or at least not encountered in our discus-
sions here (such as waves which stem from war literature,
or from what we might designate the fiction of sado-
masochism). Post-war provincial Soviet life doubles, and
alternates, with the Paris of *la belle époque* and an aspiration
to revel in and revive a *fin de siècle* style of French prose. In
diverse ways, France links with Russia, as does Siberia with
Cherbourg.

The novel contains many mentions of French writers
(especially Marcel Proust and Victor Hugo), artists and
various other cultural figures, including quoted, and much

relished, French verse. However, there are virtually no overt references to Russian writers, other than two to Nabokov (probably more as an idealised predecessor to Makine, as a cross-lingual – indeed, in Nabokov's case tri-lingual – author), and to two Symbolist poets, cited in their capacity as Russian translators of Baudelaire. The narrator, when finding himself 'between two languages', can then, he believes, 'see and feel more intensely than ever'; 'French, my "grandmother tongue", [in its *fin de siècle* form] was, I now saw, the supreme language of amazement' (*TF*, 214). France itself emerges 'from the waves' like 'a misty Atlantis' (14). Through his childhood and formative years, the narrator had remained: '[i]n search of a phantom country, a mirage of a France of yesteryear, peopled with ghosts' (171). At the same time, he began to develop himself as a genre-varying, and style-varying, raconteur.

Makine's narrative includes plentiful elements and imagery drawn from the fantastic, plus multiple assertions of absurdity. We find occurrences of music in various forms.[2] The impact of a single life (that of the grandmother figure) is of marked importance. In particular, too, time and space are played with, if, ostensibly at least, on a somewhat less than interplanetary scale. Characters, though, can identify themselves with 'extraterrestrial beings' (253), there can be 'a cosmic blunder' (143), or 'an almost cosmic alienation' can occur, with grandmother's France and her youth 'left behind in another galaxy' (206). Recollected moments formed 'a singular universe' – '[a]nother planet, almost' (228);[3] a sort of 'cosmic' travel seems to have been capable of taking place – by train or even on foot. Comets pass. Confession, perhaps not at all surprisingly, is an element within this work. Priests make a couple of brief appearances (albeit one from within Flaubert), though monks are not to be found. There are, however, two references to duelling. Moreover, a process of detection is at least a part of what is going on, and we find mention of such phenomena as spectres and alchemy. Synaesthesia frequently features. Makine's

'French fantasy' (273) condemns his protagonist, at times at least, 'to live painfully between two worlds' (196).

In Makine's French testament (itself, of course, a term with a double meaning, duly reflected in the novel) the society tale meets the narratives of 'village prose' (a post-Stalin Soviet prose movement). In something resembling Todorov's sense (referred to earlier, in Chapter 3), at least a semblance here of the detective story mingles with the historical novel, complete with metaphysical trappings, to form a metaliterary tale (and indeed a metacultural or transnational one).[4] We might even go as far as to coin the phrase 'comparativist novel' to describe Makine's testament – a generic form of which, without any doubt, other examples could be nominated, or may even have been hinted at here in the present volume.

Just one final exemplar should perhaps receive an overt mention here. Robert Bolaño's five-part novelistic saga *2666* (first published posthumously in 2004) – a highly extensive, and some might say excessive, work – includes somewhere and somehow just about all the thematic elements discussed or noted here (from the artistic story to confession and the absurd), along with many more. Furthermore, in a 'Russian literary' segment, within the final part, it even features a Russian writer who had begun his career endeavouring to write 'fifty percent', at any rate, in the manner of 'the Hoffmanian [*sic*] Odoevsky'.[5]

Notes

1 Andreï Makine, *Le Testament français* (hereafter *TF*), trans. Geoffrey Strachan, London: Sceptre, 2007 (translation first published 1997; the original was published as *Le Testament français*, Paris: Mercure de France, 1995). For a brief survey of Makine's career, see the entry on him in *The Literary Encyclopedia*: www.litencyc.com (by David Gillespie).

2 Makine is also the author of the novella *A Life's Music*, trans. Geoffrey Strachan, London: Sceptre, 2002 (*La Musique d'une vie*,

Paris: Éditions du Seuil, 2001), which does recount the life of a 'musicman'.

3 We should perhaps remember here, and particularly with the 'Starman' second chapter in mind, that the word 'planet' meant (in Greek) 'wanderer'. Salman Rushdie provides a recent reminder of this etymological fact in his latest transcultural saga: see his *The Enchantress of Florence* (London: Vintage, 2009, p. 182).

4 On the phenomenon of the 'transnational novel', see, for instance, Rachel Trousdale, '"International Fraternity": Nabokov, Chabon, and the Model Transnational', in Will Norman and Duncan White, eds, *Transitional Nabokov*, Oxford: Peter Lang, 2009, pp. 99–113.

5 Robert Bolaño, *2666*, trans. Natasha Wimmer, London: Picador, 2009, p. 711. The (fictitious) writer concerned combined this model with 'the Walter Scott disciple Lazhechnikov' (1792–1869), subsequently adding in 'the rising star Gorky' (ibid.).

Appendix

Prince Vladimir Fedorovich Odoevsky (1804–1869)

V.F. (or Vladimir) Odoevsky was the last member of a princely Russian family that traced its descent from Rurik (the Viking leader who founded Russia in the ninth century). Odoevsky is now mainly remembered, as will have been apparent here, as one of the best Russian Romantic storytellers (having been often called 'the Russian Hoffmann'), specialising in the Gothic fantastic, as well as the author of society tales and, not least, of the unusual frame-tale novel, *Russian Nights* (1844).

Odoevsky was, though, a man of many talents and careers. He held various posts in government service in St Petersburg, and finally returned to his native Moscow in the 1860s as a senator. But he was also a musical expert (even inventing his own instrument) and a keen writer of educational works for the peasants (before Leo Tolstoy did this). In addition, he was an amateur scientist, directed a major library and a museum, and spent much of his mid-life on philanthropic work. He even wrote cookery articles, under the name 'Mister Puff'. He knew all the big cultural figures: in literary life from Pushkin and the young Dostoevsky to Tolstoy; and in musical life from Glinka to the young Tchaikovsky.

After his death, comparatively little attention was paid to Odoevsky's life and work until the republications and reassessments of the twentieth century. The main exception to this situation was his unfailing popularity as an author of children's stories.

For details of works by and on Odoevsky, see the References at the ends of chapters. The translations which follow are by the present author.

Two Days in the Life of the Terrestrial Globe

There were a lot of guests at Countess B's. It was midnight, the candles were getting used up, and the conversational heat was weakening, along with the decreasing light. Already young girls were starting to talk over all the costumes for the next ball, the men had finished telling each other all the city news, the younger ladies had picked over all their acquaintances one by one, and the older ones had predicted the fates of several marriages. The gamblers had settled up amongst themselves and, having rejoined the social circle, had livened it up quite a bit with their tales of the mockery of fate, causing quite a few smiles and quite a few sighs, but soon this subject too had been exhausted. The hostess, who was extremely well versed in high-life chatter, any lull in which would be understood as boredom, was using all her skills to stir up garrulity in her tired guests. But all her efforts would have been in vain, had she not happened to glance out of the window. By good fortune, the comet was just then roaming over the starry sky and impelling astronomers to calculate, journalists to pontificate, simple folk to predict, and just about everyone else to have something to say about it. However, not one person from this entire company of gentry was as committed to it at this moment in time as Countess B. In one instant, coming to the Countess's rescue, the comet had jumped from the horizon right into her drawing room, and had forced its way through an unbelievable quantity of hats and bonnets – to be greeted by a similarly immeasurable quantity of different comments, some humorous and some regrettable. Some people were indeed afraid that this comet would play tricks on them; others, laughing, were convinced that it augured some wedding, or some divorce, and so on and so forth.

'You must be joking,' said one of the guests, who had spent his whole life in society, engaged in astronomy (*par originalité*), 'you may joke, but I remember one astronomer declaring that comets can come very close to the Earth, even collide with it – and then it would be no joke at all.'

'Oh! How terrible!' the ladies cried. 'But tell us, what would happen then, when a comet hits the Earth? Will the Earth fall down?' several voices muttered.

'The Earth will be shattered to bits,' said the society astronomer.

'Oh, my God! And so that's when the social world will really be seen for what it is,' said one rather aged lady.

'Rest assured,' replied the astronomer, 'other scientists maintain that this cannot happen, and that the Earth gets one degree nearer to the Sun every hundred and fifty years and that the day will finally come when the Earth will get burned up by the Sun.'

'Oh, stop, do stop,' cried the ladies. 'How awful!'

The astronomer's words attracted widespread attention; at this point, endless arguments began. There were no disasters, at that moment, to which the terrestrial globe was not being subjected. They were burning it in fire, drowning it in water, and all of this was being affirmed, of course, not through the testimony of any scientists, but by quoting the utterances of some dear deceased uncle, who had been a chamberlain, or some late aunt, who had been a lady of state, and so on.

'Listen,' the hostess finally exclaimed, 'instead of arguing about it, let's, every one of us, write down on a piece of paper our thoughts on the subject, and then – why don't we all guess who wrote down this or that opinion?'

'Oh, yes! Yes, let's all write something,' all the guests shouted. . .

'How do you want us to write it?' asked one young man timidly. 'In French, or in Russian?'

'*Fi donc – mauvais genre!*' said the hostess. 'Who in this day and age writes in French? *Messieurs et Mesdames!* You have to write in Russian.'

Paper was given out. Many sat down there and then at the table, but a lot of people, realising that things were stretching to an ink-well and to the Russian language, whispered into their neighbours' ear that there were still a number of visits to be made – and promptly disappeared.

When the writing had been finished, all the bits of paper were mixed up, and each person in turn read out their allotted piece. What follows is one of these conjectures, which seemed to us more remarkable than the rest, and which we here impart to our readers.

I

It had come about. The destruction of the terrestrial globe had begun. The astronomers have pronounced; the people's voice corroborates their view. This voice is implacable; it faithfully fulfils its promises. This comet, unprecedented until now, at an immeasurable speed accelerates towards the Earth. The sun only has to go down for this dreadful *wayfarer* to flare up. Delights are forgotten, misfortunes are forgotten, passions are stilled, desires have faded; there is neither peace nor activity, neither sleep nor wakefulness. Both day and night people of all callings, in all conditions, lament upon the squares, and their trembling, pale faces are illuminated by a crimson flame.

Huge towers were turned into an observatory. Day and night the gazes of astronomers were fixed on the sky. Everyone came running to them, as though to all-powerful gods. Their words went flying from mouth to mouth. Astronomy was turning into the popular science. Everyone was doing calculations of the size of the comet, and the speed of its motion. They were thirsting for mistakes in the astronomers' computations, but didn't find them.

'Look here, just look,' one person said, 'yesterday it was no bigger than the Moon, but now it's twice the size. . . what's it going to be like tomorrow?'

'Tomorrow it'll run into the Earth and crush us,' said another. . .

'Couldn't we go off to the other side of the globe?' said a third person.

'Couldn't we construct defensive positions, to repulse it with machines?' said a fourth. 'What is the government thinking about?'

'There's no way out!' shouted one young man, out of puff. 'I've just come from the tower – the scientists are saying that, even before it runs into the Earth, there will be storms, earth-quakes and the surface will be ablaze. . .'

'Who will stand against the anger of God?' exclaimed one elder.

Meanwhile time moves on and with it grow the size of the comet and public alarm as well. It is now getting visibly bigger. In the day, the sun shuts it out; at night it hangs over the Earth as a fiery cleft. Already a silent, awesome certainty had given way to despair. Neither groan nor lamentation was to be heard. The prisons were opened: the freed prisoners wander among the crowds with drooping heads. Rarely, only rarely, are the silence and the inaction interrupted: there's the cry of an infant who has been left without food, but then he will be silent again, admiring the awful heavenly spectacle; or now a father embraces the killer of his son.

But when the wind blows or thunder resounds, the crowd will start to stir – and everyone's lips are ready to mouth the question, but they fear to utter it.

In a secluded street of one European city an eighty-year-old man at his domestic hearth was cooking himself some food: suddenly his son runs in to him.

'What are you doing, father?' he exclaims.

'What should I be doing?' the old man replies calmly. 'You've all left – you're running about the streets, whereas I just go hungry. . .'

'Father! Is it really the time now to be thinking about food?'

'It's also exactly the time, as it always is. . .'

'But our destruction. . .'

'Calm down. This groundless fear will pass, as do all earthly calamities. . .'

'But have you really completely lost your hearing and your vision?'

'Quite the opposite; not only have I preserved both, but also something above that, which you don't have: peace of spirit and strength of reason. Calm down, I say to you. The comet just appeared unexpectedly and will disappear likewise; and the destruction of the Earth is not at all as imminent as you think.

The Earth has still not achieved maturity. . . an inner feeling assures me of that. . .'

'My dear father! Your whole life you've had a stronger belief in this feeling, or in your daydreams, than in reality! Are you really, even now, going to remain dedicated to imagination?'

'The fear that I can see on your face, and the faces of those like you! This shabby fear is not compatible with the profound moment of demise. . .'

'How dreadful!' exclaimed the young man. 'My father has completely lost his reason. . .'

At that same instant a terrible thunderbolt shook the territory, lightning flared, rain deluged down, a gale removed roofs from the buildings – the population threw themselves to the ground. . .

The night passed, the sky brightened, and a gentle Zephyr had dried the ground, which had been awash with rain. . . the people did not dare to raise their lowered heads; eventually they did take the liberty. They by now feel themselves to be in the guise of bodiless spirits. . . Finally they stand up and look about them: the same familiar places, the same bright sky, the same people. An involuntary motion lifts everyone's gaze to the sky: the comet was moving away from the skyline.

II

This brought on a collective feast of the terrestrial globe. There was no tempestuous joy at this feast; nor were loud ejaculations heard! Long since had lively merriment turned for them into silent delight, into the usual round. Long since had they stepped over the obstacles preventing a human being from being a human being. The memory had already gone of the times when crude matter could laugh at the efforts of the spirit, when need gave way to necessity. The times of imperfection and prejudice had long since passed, together with human diseases. The planet was the mighty dwelling place of only the most powerful tsars, so no one was surprised at nature's magnificent feast. Everyone awaited it, for long had the premonition of it appeared to the imagination of the chosen ones in the form of a delightful vision. No one asked others anything about it; a triumphant thought shone across all faces and everyone could understand this mute eloquence. Quietly, the Earth drew near to the Sun, and an unburning warmth, like a fire of inspiration, extended across it. Just another moment – and the heavenly became the earthly, the earthly the heavenly: the Sun became the Earth and the Earth the Sun. . .

(1825)

The Witness

(dedicated to A.I. Koshelev)

. . . I jumped out of my carriage and kissed my native soil. The sound of a Russian Orthodox Church bell recalled me from that feeling of self-oblivion which overcomes the soul at the sight of the fatherland, specially after a separation from it of ten years. Not too far away, on a hillock, the walls of a monastery shone white. My tiredness forgotten, I rushed to the open gates of the place of worship, not with the cool curiosity of a traveller, but just as the infant rushes to the maternal embrace. This is every-one's experience, following a lengthy separation from the motherland.

Vespers had gone. Through the semicircular windows came the drawn out, crimson rays of the setting sun, playing in the clouds of church incense, settling in tiers on the gleaming gilt of the iconostasis – like a long, bitter prayer, stirred up by bloody passions, finally getting through to the awning sur-rounding the testament of the soul. The fresh evening air was percolating through the opened doors. Villagers were starting to leave the church; after them, in a black stream, stretched the monastic brethren. I remained stationary; the deserted church seemed to me even more majestic, even more auspicious. Its appearance promoted the kind of thoughts that disappear amidst a crowd, in the middle of stormy life, and which cannot be caught in words, but which speak so distinctly to the heart. An almost inaudible rustle made me aware that I was not alone. In a distant corner I noticed a monk stretched out on a cold platform. An involuntary curiosity compelled me also to stay in the church. Eventually the recluse stood up; his face lit up in the rays of the sun.

The unknown figure seemed to recognise me as well. We came closer.

'Is that you, Rostislav?'

'Is that you, Grigorii?' – and we clasped each other around the neck. I recognised my old friend from active service, my old boyhood friend.

'What does that garb signify? What is the meaning of your pale, exhausted face? Is that you, the bold hussar, the star of the Petersburg balls?'

The monk did not answer a word, but sighed deeply and led me to his cell. This is what he told me:

'Shortly after your departure to other lands I went off on leave to see my family. At home I found my mother, who was already very weak and ill. I barely recognised my younger brother: at his age, a person changes so quickly – and I hadn't seen him for five years. He was now about seventeen; he was a good-looking boy and was of a very pleasant youthful disposition. Mother didn't want to let go of him. He was the one child of hers that she had fed herself, and you know how that relation-ship can produce between mother and child some sort of a mysterious, indissoluble, almost physical bond, which strength-ens in the highest degree what is in any case a fervent maternal feeling, and does not disappear with the years. Viacheslav would have acceded completely to his mother's wishes. But once he had seen my splendid uniform, my moustache, and heard the stories about my regimental friends, the theatre, and all the enjoyments of Petersburg life – he forgot about his moth-er's wishes and his promises, and he began persistently asking her for permission to enter military service. To his entreaties I added my own. I described to our mother all the advantages that this way of life would bring him. I reminded her that we would each be there in support of the other; I promised that I would be permanently close to Viacheslav, to be for him not only a brother, but a father. After a drawn-out tussle, she called me over alone to her couch and said to me:

"I am no longer able to resist your supplications. I do not wish for my children ever to be able to accuse me of preventing their happiness in life. Take Viacheslav with you. But, Rostislav, do not rejoice in my consent. You cannot comprehend the responsibility I am imposing on you. If I were able to get from this couch to the carriage, I would travel with you, but that would do no good. To me, in my state, it's all the same, whether it's seven hundred kilometres or seventeen metres: there's no way I would keep up with you. I would only be a hindrance to you in life, and you know that I do not belong to that category of mothers who, through some form of egoism, love to keep their children tied to them by a leash, knowing full well how utterly bored they are. Now, just listen: Viacheslav is an infant. He doesn't know himself what he wants, he doesn't know people, or life. But you, Rostislav, you are no longer a child. You have got through that stage of awful crisis when a person doesn't have in the head a single thought of his own, when one cannot really be aware of anything, when any word spoken louder than the last one may lead one away from the straight and narrow. Naturally, you will have a strong influence on your brother. For a long time yet he will be thinking with your head, feeling with your heart, and living through your life. Take care of yourself, and take care of him. I won't accept from you any excuses – for whatever he does, you will be responsible to me. In your dealings with your brother you must foresee everything, warn him of everything, and you will be answerable to me for his behaviour – both in this life, and in the next."

These words are still sounding in my ears even now. Mother was deeply moved – and I was as well. In my heart I was firmly convinced that her trust in me was not at all misplaced, and I took a harrowing oath that I would fulfil her sacred bidding.

The end of my leave was approaching, and we pulled ourselves away from our mother's embraces. Viacheslav I had to get into the carriage almost unconscious: he was crying like a child.

I am not going to describe to you the first years of our Petersburg life. I could not complain about Viacheslav. He was a bit frivolous, but still maintained a completely chaste soul, such a rare thing these days among young people. Trifling things upset him; and trifles amused him. He was all on the surface, saying anything that came into his head. At a happy moment he would jump on to tables and chairs; at a sad time he could not hold back the tears. Sometimes, for hours at a time, he would run around the room with Boksen, his young setter; and then he would say that they loved each other for being of the same character, for the one was just as mad as the other. And indeed, Boksen, who wouldn't even let me near him, allowed Viacheslav to do everything with him that entered his empty head; and when, as used to happen, they got carried away by their playing, I had to summon up all my composure so as not to burst out laughing, or to get really angry. But, I must confess, I preferred my brother's childish simplicity to the premature guardedness of some of his comrades, who, it seemed, must have been diplomats in their cradles. I introduced him to quite a number of ladies; and I took him to balls. He danced diligently, with full and open enjoyment. His cheerful and transparent appearance could not help but please: the ladies ran after him without mercy, taking him for a complete child, and he, the prankster, as they say *faisait le gros dos*.[1] I took a pride in him, watching him at it, like a father watching his infant.

Eventually the long and impatiently awaited day arrived: Viacheslav was commissioned with the rank of cornet. To imagine his joy is impossible. Unfamiliar with the decorous pretence of today's young men, he twirled himself unceasingly in front of the mirror, first to this side and then to that, in order the better to be able to see his epaulettes. Then he rushed over to embrace me, then he put on his three-cornered hat; then he dragged Boksen around by the paws. "Do you know, Boksen," he said, "that I am now a cornet? Do you understand that? Do you realise that now you'll be walking along Nevsky Prospect with me, with your master, the cornet?. . ." And it did seem as though Boksen understood him; at least he wagged his tail and answered Viacheslav's words with a loud bark. All these simple

---

1 Gave himself airs (*Fr.*) [author's note].

incidences in our then life, all these words of Viacheslav's, are so alive in my memory.'

Tears rolled down from the recluse's eyelashes. He took a deep breath, and then seemed engrossed, probably trying to gather his thoughts; eventually he went on:

'One of our comrades, Vetsky, had an elder brother, working in the civil service. I liked him a lot; he was a man of quite remarkable intelligence, but I don't think I have ever seen a more awkward man. He had been physically somehow premature and from that suffered from very poor health. He was fully aware of his physical debility and for that reason permitted himself no excesses – not even any gymnastic exercises. He walked slowly, taking care with every step. His riding was such that no horseman could look at him without laughing. When the younger people pranced around at a fiery gallop, he would timidly enquire as to which was the most placid horse and painstakingly examine whether its girth had been properly strapped. Moreover, he had some sort of a speech impediment, which gave him a kind of drawl, almost a stammer. You can imagine the effect he produced in a young crowd of skilled riders, full of life and dash, often extending to recklessness.

Vetsky was a good companion. He was liked, but everyone considered it an obligation to make fun of him, of his delicate physique, his inhibitions, and his caution, which often stretched to timidity. Vetsky tolerated all these taunts with the greatest composure. Sometimes he would get out of things with a witty quip, and sometimes he would join in the laugh at his own expense, but more often he wouldn't know what to reply to unexpected sallies, for it seemed that his mental capabilities could be just as inhibited as his physical ones. He belonged to that category of people easily knocked from their stride if words are slung at them, and who will often be at a complete loss for the first minute or two. But such a position was not a pleasant one for Vetsky, although he tried to cover his anger beneath an ever calm and cool exterior. It was obvious that he was expending every effort not to lose control of himself, repeating with a smile that getting angry made him *unwell*. After a while, I noticed that my brother made fun of Vetsky more than anyone, but we were all so used to laughing at our *tail-coat wearer*, so used to seeing him as an amusing distraction, that I didn't pay special attention to my brother's behaviour. It just seemed so natural to all of us. The thing was, as I found out afterwards, that Viacheslav became jealous of Vetsky over a certain beauty who, through some strange caprice, preferred our awkward eccentric to my skilful, handsome horseman.

New officers had to, as they say, *wet their epaulettes*. They took days sorting it all out, so as to organise a bash, first for one of them, then for another, but the rapid exodus of the regiments from barracks into the Petersburg environs compelled them to postpone their binges until such time as they would have moved completely into summer quarters. Finally the bingeing days began. You cannot have any conception of these. Ten years is an entire age in Russia. Gone are the days of the crude, unbridled orgies, which you can still remember. Young people now are in their senses, even after a bottle of wine. Today's orgies are orderly, respectable ones. A woman can attend them without blushing. But, despite that, as of old, champagne still has its effect on people, and blood will still go to the head from it. It may be true that now, they say, it's no longer a matter of honour to drink oneself under the table, but, in the old way, from wine a man becomes merrier, quicker, unpredictable in his moves and, in the old way, all his feelings become keener. Every thought, otherwise lying forgotten deep in the soul in a sober state, will magnify under a soaking of champagne, as though under a microscope.

This spree took place in a fairly small wooden country house. They didn't stint on the champagne. Moreover, this spree was not the first one, and everyone's head, even that of Vetsky, was, as they used to say, at least half-cocked. It got to two o'clock in the morning. I felt suffocated, so I left the villa, and walked off around the countryside. As I now recall it, the night was a cool and bright one. With delight I drank in the fresh air, and admired the village view, which was already beginning to glow crimson from the first rays of dawn. It was quiet all round, but just one little house was lit up – the one with the feasting going on. Shadows scuttled across the windows; guffaws and the merry shouts of young people reached me.

Suddenly. . . everything went quiet. I unwittingly shuddered at this sudden silence. My heart started beating strongly, just as though I had just heard some dreadfully bad news. Without being aware of my feelings, I involuntarily doubled my step on my way back to the villa. When I walked in, my foreboding proved justified. Inside the doorway I ran straight into Vetsky, a sword in his hands. He didn't say a word to me, but was as white as a sheet, and was anxious to conceal an inner agitation under his indifferent smile.

I was told straight away what had happened in my absence: a frivolous, childish prank, but one which had to have a bloody end. . .

The young people had opened the window on to the yard. One of them took it into his head to jump out from it, and then another, and then a third one. Anyone falling would hurt himself, because the window was quite a high one. Amid general laughter, the risk aroused in the young folk a strange sense of self-esteem: everyone wanted to give it a try – would anyone break his neck in the course of this exploit?

"Well, how about you, then?" my brother had said to the older Vetsky, with a mocking smile.

"I am not intending to jump," Vetsky replied coldly.

"That's no good! You've really got to jump."

"I told you, I don't want to."

"You don't want to jump," my brother replied, flushed with wine, "because you're a coward."

"I wouldn't advise you to repeat those words," said Vetsky.

My poor brother himself didn't remember what he said, or what he did.

"Not only will I repeat them," he retorted, hands on hips, "but I shall make a point of telling Countess M——" (the lady that both were running after), "I shall say to her: your tender admirer he's a coward! Do you want to bet I don't?"

Vetsky, notwithstanding all his capacity for composure, completely lost his temper. He grabbed my brother roughly by the arm and muttered:

"Just you dare, you lunatic!"

A blow with a glove across the face was the reply.

What now was to be done? For a time I thought about reconciling the opponents, but how? Forcing my brother to apologise would be impossible: his pride had been inflamed by his officer's uniform. He realised himself that he had acted stupidly, but to begin his career with what he would have called an unworthy trick, to get cold feet – to this he would not agree. I myself at that time could not envisage this other than with horror. It remained for me to work on Vetsky. I was counting on his constant timidity, on his constant caution and good sense. At that moment of egoism, it seemed to me that it would cost nothing to leave this man under a yoke of universal scorn, just in order to save my brother. Restraining my own sense of pride, I went off to see our tail-coated civil servant.

When I entered his room, he was sitting at his writing table and calmly smoking a cigar. His composure alarmed me.

"I wanted to speak," I said to him, "not with your second, but with you. You, as an intelligent man, must really see in my brother's behaviour nothing other than the prank of a mere boy, who doesn't merit your attention."

Vetsky gave me a look of surprise and replied with a smile.

"You can believe," he said, "that I, more than anyone, regret your brother's behaviour. But allow me to say to you: you yourself are not thinking about what you're saying: just tell me this – can this really be left without attention?"

These few words changed my way of thinking about Vetsky. I wanted to touch his inner feelings. I related to him all our family circumstances – our farewell to Mother, her words. . . I made no effort to spare Viacheslav, calling him a crazy, retarded child; I even uttered the word *pardon*.

"Allow me to ask you," Vetsky said to me, with his usual cold smile, "are you offering me an apology in your brother's name, or in your own?"

I was embarrassed and didn't know what to say to him. He fixed me with a penetrating look.

"I quite understand your position. I know that your brother will not apologise to me, and that it's not possible for him to apologise to me. I really sympathise with you, and even with him. I am no swashbuckler; duels are not my business. My rule in life has been always to avoid giving cause for any such thing, but," he added emphatically, "never to back off, even a step, when danger is unavoidable. Put yourself in my position: how many times have I let go as jokes those sort of words from your brother, which from anyone else would have caused a couple of dozen duels? I spared him for his youth, and I can admit to you, I spared myself, for in life there are quite enough unpleasantnesses without that. And life is short: why sacrifice it over trivialities? But this is a more serious matter. Just think, yourself, what would become of me if, in addition to the generally held opinion about my excessive cautiousness, I should leave the present incident, as you put it, without attention? You know about society's prejudices: I would find no quarter anywhere on the globe. Fingers would be pointed at me. My only recourse would be to shoot myself, but that, you must agree, would be in contradiction to my *cautiousness.*"

These words were cold, plain and derisive. In accordance with my precepts at that time, I could not refute them.

"If that's the way it is," I shouted back heatedly, "then, my dear sir, you will be having dealings with me."

"If that be your pleasure," replied Vetsky, flicking off the ash from his cigar, "but not before we have concluded our dealings with your little brother. However, you know yourself that, anyway, your brother, in all probability, would not agree to any such arrangement. Now, excuse me – I now have a number of letters to finish."

With these words, he made a cold bow. I rushed out of the room with a feeling of despair in my heart.

Back in my quarters, Vetsky's second was waiting for me. He announced that he was charged not to agree to any proposals of reconciliation, except the one – that my brother should agree to apologise to Vetsky before the entire regimental officer corps. I don't know about now, but certainly then, such a condition seemed completely impossible.

One last hope remained: Vetsky couldn't shoot. I, in accordance with the precepts of the time, was my brother's natural second; I was the closest to him and such an undertaking seemed to me the inevitable duty of kinship and friendship. Thinking through all the conditions that might give some advantage to my brother, I proposed that they should fire at twenty paces, with the first to shoot remaining at the barrier. I was relying on my brother's marksmanship. Vetsky's second willingly accepted my proposal. Hardly had we concluded this homicidal arrangement, when Viacheslav walked in. Boksen was jumping about in front of him with a joyful bark. My brother was trying to display a lack of concern and full composure. He played and jumped about with his dog as always, but I could see that inwardly he was anxious. Probably life was dangling itself before the youth in all its delights. Most certainly he didn't want to part with it. I looked at his fresh and handsome face, and my heart just bled. In those few hours I aged twenty years.

Within a few minutes we were already at the place. The idea that I had brought my brother to within range of a lead bullet dominated all my capacities for thought and action. In vain did I wish to display the composure required for such occasions – I was quite beside myself. Vetsky's second had to carry out my duties. The decisive minute arrived. I tried to muster all my powers. I inspected Viacheslav's pistol. They were standing in their places. Vetsky was as cold as ice: a barely noticeable smile was visible on his clenched lips. It was as though he was standing by the fireplace at a dazzling reception. Glancing at Viacheslav, I noticed with horror that his hand was shaking.

The signal was given. The opponents slowly began to approach one another. . . The appearance of danger made Viacheslav forget all my advice – he fired. . . Vetsky wobbled, but he did not fall; the bullet had smashed his left shoulder.

Concealing his pain, he signalled to Viacheslav to approach the barrier. With an involuntary convulsive movement, my brother obeyed. . .

At that moment I froze to the spot; a cold sweat poured down me. I could see the slow approach of Vetsky, his aiming of the murderous cocking-piece, and I could see Vetsky's calm, inexorable expression. Now he was just two paces from my brother. I remembered Mother, her words and my promises, and I got into a state close to madness. It all went black, and I lost sense of everything: honour, conscience and the rules of society. I remembered just one thing: that *they were killing my brother right in front of me. . .* I couldn't bear this instant, and I threw myself at Viacheslav, grabbed him, shielded him with my own body, and shouted to Vetsky:

"Go on, shoot!"

Vetsky lowered his pistol.

"Is that really in the conditions agreed for the duel?" he said, calmly turning to his second.

A general cry of disapproval resounded from among those present. I was dragged away from my brother. . . A shot rang out – and Viacheslav dropped as though dead!

How can I tell you what was going on with me at that moment? I tore myself away from those holding me, rushed to Viacheslav and, unconscious of anything, looked at his grievous, dying torments. I saw his eyes closing for ever!. . . At this same instant, Boksen, on his broken lead, ran up to the bloody spot, landed on Viacheslav, howled and licked at his wound.

This sight brought me back to myself. I leaped over, and grabbed at the pistol, but Vetsky, weakened from his wound, was already lying unconscious on a stretcher. Burning for vengeance, I would have thrown myself at the wounded man, ready to tear him to pieces, but the others stopped me. . . As though through a dream, there rang in my ears reproaches and condemnations from my fellow-officers. . .'

'What more is there to tell you?' the recluse went on. 'You know about the consequences of duels. But the punishment for my misdemeanour to me was nothing: my punishment was in my heart. My life was at an end. I wished for only one thing: either to lose my unneeded life in battle with an enemy, or to bury myself alive. I was not favoured with the first honour. Here, far from my native parts, not known to anyone, I am trying through lamentation and sorrow to stifle the voice of my own heart. But to this day dreadful visions awaken me at night. . . my mother, dying in despair. . . and in my ears ring the terrible words of the scripture: *"Cain, where is thy brother?"* '

(1839)

Index